A CALL TO FURTHER BECOMING

A Call to Further Becoming

The New Declaration from
WOMEN OVER 50

SUE MARCHNER BRIGHTMAN

HOUNDSTOOTH
PRESS

A CALL TO FURTHER BECOMING

The New Declaration from Women Over 50

ISBN   978-1-5445-0683-8 *Hardcover*

978-1-5445-0682-1 *Paperback*

978-1-5445-0681-4 *Ebook*

To Lilly and Sam, the loves of my life, whose continued unfolding fills me with joy and awe.

And to every one of us endeavoring to become more of who we really are and doing what is ours to do.

CONTENTS

"God expresses in man the infinite idea forever developing itself, broadening and rising higher and higher from a boundless basis."

—MARY BAKER EDDY

INTRODUCTION

There are times of rising. And for women well over fifty, this is one of them.

At this moment in history, women are redefining what it means to be alive and "continuing to become" at a stage of life previously called the autumn (read: dying) of our years. Gone are the days of going gently into the night, going grey, or going away.

We are here. And we're not going back.

We are here and we're continuing to grow: physically, mentally, professionally, spiritually. In every colorful way readers can imagine.

We are here contributing on the political stage, the performance stage, the educational stage, the research stage, the corporate stage.

We are here launching businesses that we've secretly envisioned in our hearts for decades.

We are here liberating our creativity—through painting, singing, acting, photographing, writing, and dancing.

We are here pioneering on every front possible, including new ways to travel and serve along the way; new ways to invest in meaningful relationships; and new ways to define intergenerational family-ing.

We are here proclaiming, initiating, and advocating beauty in the world—not showy, artificial or commercialized beauty, but pure, soul-stirring, authentic beauty.

We are here running marathons and declaring new rules for winning.

We are here honoring the decades of women before us who had far fewer choices, while also living large in our freedom and experimentation in ways they could not.

We are here building mentorships with younger women in our quest to share the hard-earned lessons we hope they don't have to repeat.

We are here retiring the word "retirement"—or at least its meaningless definitions from yesteryear.

We are here to further the evolution of goodness in the world.

And we have the backbone to do it.

What this looks like for every woman is as different as millions of grains of sand under a microscope and magnified 300 times: sublime beyond imagination, each a different color, history, shape; contoured by the rumbling waves that brought us to stretching shores across time. None can ever be replicated, and each has an essence that contributes to the grand whole, exquisite and timeless.

Whomever you are and wherever you are in your life journey, let this be your takeaway:

Women over fifty—and especially those in their sixties and seventies—are not on a downward arc of any kind. We are, in fact, rising.

This book is dedicated to the rising.

A NEW BLUEPRINT FOR THIS STAGE OF LIFE

A Call to Further Becoming: The New Declaration from Women Over 50 identifies ten themes representing who we are and what we are learning as we're living it.

Yes. At the same time we're walking it, we're beginning to define the rising.

We are here putting off the old narrative and putting on the new. Rewriting our identities and storylines. It's not because women over fifty consciously decided to *demand* a new narrative, but more that we're *already* living and experiencing it, whether *we* are aware of it or not.

This pioneering spirit and irresistible impulse to redefine our purpose and ourselves at this stage is crucially important to name and claim.

I began to recognize unmistakable signs of this massive shift several years ago when I was in my mid-fifties. Whether I was at home in Colorado or traveling internationally for work, a trend began to present itself: my female friends, colleagues, international coaching clients, as well as women in workshops I was facilitating were all deeply questioning conventional post-career models of life.

I discovered many of us over fifty were not the least bit interested in retirement in its traditional forms. Many of us did not have the option or desire to stop earning. And many of us wanted to complete former career paths and move on to something different (more creative, meaningful, satisfying). We no longer believed the once-unquestioned arc of diminished options that lay ahead after working successfully in impressive careers.

Instead, we were—and still are—living the question, "What now?"

In fact, we're living a *myriad* of new questions. Who are we at this age? What's possible? What are we being called to do? Why the unrest we feel?

Once I committed to this book and started interviewing women over fifty, I found the questions became even wider in scope: How do we channel our well-informed wisdom into a world that seems to be calling for a whole new form of leading and living? What do we want this stage of life to be, for ourselves and in service to the greater good?

As I heard these questions being asked by hundreds of women with whom I came into contact, I was also hearing *desires* from women in the over-fifty age range. The themes were resoundingly similar:

- Strong inclinations to continue contributing in the world, but not in the same way.
- Restlessness fueled by physical and intellectual vibrancy, with long lives ahead and no desire to "wind down."
- Creative interests re-emerging that had been put on a back shelf for decades.
- An attraction to experimenting.

- Intolerance for…well, *many* things.
- Freedom from the need for recognition or further achievement and the new spaciousness that brings.
- A desire for spiritual exploration and development.
- Quality relationships as a nonnegotiable priority.

WE'RE ENTERING A TIME OF WILDERNESS

Having studied change and transition for thirty years as an organizational development consultant and leadership coach, working globally in numerous business settings, I've come to see how transitions both large scale and small usually begin with an ending.

Something comes to completion (though not always planned)—something we've outgrown or seen beyond in our evolving ways of being. Then there's a wilderness period before we reach the new beginning.

This wilderness period is often disorienting as old models and paradigms begin to disintegrate and an old sense of identity fades, but a new one has not become apparent. It's also marked by distinct feelings of aloneness at times, and a lack of concrete handrails to grip in the dark. We often don't choose the unsettling territory of a wilderness—especially when we don't know what it might include and didn't take the course (if there was one!) on how to make it through safely. Though I see this as specific to the new ways women are experiencing and redefining life after fifty, I believe we can also see how the whole world is very much in a wilderness phase right now—as so many familiar structures and beliefs are crumbling and needing to be re-formed.

The good news is, wilderness periods are ripe for creativity, curiosity, and the forging of new ways to create the future we want for ourselves personally—and also collectively. We can greet these transitions with expectancy, a feeling of opportunity, and attraction to what may emerge in the newness.

Given the importance of the profound shift I sensed happening with women in the fifty to seventy-plus stage of life, I set out on a discovery to find out more about the burning questions I was hearing from others and experiencing in my own life. That is why, beginning in 2016, I decided to interview 100 women over age fifty.

With forty years of interviewing experience—first as a children's protective services investigator, then a social worker certifying foster homes, then a Human Resources manager, and finally for most of my career an organizational consultant conducting corporate culture surveys and large-scale diagnostic assessments, I knew how to craft thoughtful questions.

More than that, I've always loved *listening*.

I never would have guessed that the new territory I was exploring—in my case through interviewing these 100 women—would be my way out of my own wilderness and into a whole new arena of creative work—that of offering this map called a Declaration of Further Becoming for the women who suddenly find themselves here.

ABOUT THE WOMEN YOU'LL MEET

The majority of the 100 women I interviewed for this book have been at the top of their game across various professions and what had been glass ceilings, glass walls, and glass entry doors. From them and from others who have walked different paths, I wanted to hear what's happening at this stage as we approach a massive transition and redefine what it means to be over fifty. I wanted to hear them speak about the new tracks we're laying down as we each take new steps in our individual lives and begin to witness the new emerging pattern.

As I stepped into the interview process, I had specific questions I wanted to explore:

- What's happening in the lives of women age fifty-plus, especially those who have had strongly defined careers over the last few decades and are facing a major work-life transition?
- What's common? What's not?
- How are we navigating the big "what now" question, especially as we enter our sixties?
- Is traditional retirement (travel, volunteering, relaxation, ease) a thing of the past?
- What's most important at this stage of life?
- What are we learning as we navigate this new territory that might support other women?
- And what answers might all of this reveal to the world at large?

Every woman I interviewed was wonderfully generous with her life lessons and learnings as we explored these topics. I felt, and still feel, deeply privileged to have heard each woman's story.

A few more facts about the interviewees. They were all between fifty-one and ninety-three, with the large majority in their mid-fifties to late seventies. The 100 women also represent diversities of race, religion, upbringing, professional background, marital status, and economic levels. They hail from all parts of the US and from Western Europe with a few interviewees from India, Mexico, Australia, and Madagascar. They include Caucasian,

Latina, African American, African, Indian, and Native American women.

In terms of socioeconomics, some interviewees had periods of time where poverty was at their doorstep, but none lived in chronic poverty. However, the anxiety of low wages and/or the inconsistency of income was a reality for some. Others enjoyed salaries at the top of earning scales and would appear, to many, as 1 percenters. The majority fall squarely in the category of middle to upper-middle class. Some are married; some divorced or widowed; some remarried, some single; some gay; some satisfied not identifying in any category related to relationships.

I didn't intend to conduct "hard" research, per se. For example, not all continents are represented, nor are distinctly rural lifestyles represented nearly as much as city/town residencies.

Also, I haven't tried to identify distinctions for subgroups within the 100 women, such as responses specifically from those outside the US or from specific ethnicities. I allowed women to speak directly to the questions I asked and to tell their stories in their own words. Where women mentioned economic level, religion, or race as a key part of a quote, I tried to keep the integrity of that context when quoting them.

My deepest thanks to these 100 remarkable women who helped make this Declaration possible; who trusted me with their stories and allowed me to hold them with integrity for all to hear.

HOW MY DISCOVERIES EMERGED

The due diligence I applied in order to accurately identify key themes from the 100 interviews had numerous precise steps that eventually led to this book and the Declaration it represents.

First was collating every response to every question from 100 one-hour phone interviews. I took verbatim notes; a skill I learned long ago for which I'm enormously grateful. I then mapped them into similar threads or groupings per question. Following, the groupings were organized by decades (fifties, sixties, seventies) so I could identify significant differences per ten-year period. I took great care not to name a main headline or theme too early. (There's a reason my coaching colleagues once dubbed me *Precision*.)

Sometimes during the mapping process, after carefully studying a pattern of responses, I recognized a further, more specific split of one into two themes. For example, in capturing and tracking what women shared as nonnegotiable practices in their lives—a specific question I asked—I noticed the majority of women mentioned some type of prayer practice. As I studied this, it became clear that prayer and meditation were two distinct activities and that "walking in nature"—mentioned by some women as a prayer practice—was a third category. I paid close attention to these differences. They fascinated me. I felt it was important to reflect all the elegance and nuance of the 100 interviews. In a word, it was about integrity.

Occasionally a theme emerged that had immediately-clear sub-themes. One example is the Declaration called "Self-Witnessing in Solitude" with its rich, distinct sub-themes about how the 100 women practice this in ways deeply meaningful to them.

As I listened and studied the responses, I started discovering fascinating themes that were not direct responses to questions but were statistically significant. For instance, the Declaration "Done With That" is an example of an unmistakable pronouncement that emerged, though not in response to a specific question about it. These were thrilling for me to hear, because they arose unexpectedly and totally independent from the focus of any given question. Long ago, I learned as an interviewer that themes of importance to the interviewee will eventually come out, no matter the questions. We just have to listen.

I do not intend to assert that if something didn't emerge as a theme, it isn't important to women over age fifty—or to these 100 women. It simply didn't emerge with consistency, or at all. In short, I listened for similarities—clear themes of statistical significance in my 700 pages of notes from 100 one-hour phone interviews—using a rigorous process learned in my corporate background.

That said, I allowed many months of reflection about what women did *not* say. For example, the phrase "bucket list" did not come up even once. (My take? Women over fifty want to live fully now, not later.) Women also did not mention finding a life partner as a priority, which surprised me. Again, this does not necessarily mean this isn't important to women over fifty, or to these 100 women. It does mean that when responding about priorities, practices, advice to other women, stepping-stones that helped them become who they are today and similar questions, seeking a life partner was not mentioned with any statistical significance.

THE DISTINCTIONS BETWEEN DECADES

One of the biggest breakthroughs of awareness for me came from separating responses by decades. I was able to hear what women in their fifties are saying distinct from women in their sixties (a big difference), and women in their sixties as somewhat distinct from women in their seventies.

Whereas the fifties seem to be a hard-charging completion of what's taken place up to this decade, with a significant reckoning toward the end of those ten years, it appears to be our sixties and seventies where the biggest change is taking place. For those who are over sixty, there seems to be a whole new way of being that we're discovering, however confusing it might be to those of us pioneering what is not yet completely defined.

Women interviewees in their fifties, however, oftentimes had one or both feet still in the professional arena into which they had already poured much energy. I certainly did. So, the counsel flowing from women in later decades encouraged women in their fifties to make full use of the intensely focused steam still available for whatever full-on push might light them up. There was a rally cry of "Go for it!"

Women who had reached the sixties and beyond referred to the fifties as "the decade you've been working up to;" "a time to do what you've always wanted, full on." Recommendations came loudly and enthusiastically for women in their fifties to give themselves the gift of full permission to go for what they really want. Getting a coach, finding ways to strengthen the gifts they most want to use, and seeking help in whatever way would support fulfilling the dreams they'd been working toward were all mentioned as important considerations.

Several women said their fifties was the decade within which they reached their highest professional achievements; a time when they could enjoy the fruits of all their hard work and feel the spaciousness of claiming their mastery. One woman used the phrase "the fabulous fifties"—and offered the view that we should begin to embrace the idea that something is still to come up ahead. Just the *idea* of a next phase of adventure is important to claim! This is when we begin to replace the ridiculous notion that we're coming to a hill, going over the hill—or that there even is a hill.

Woman after woman spoke to me of the grand possibilities of the fifth decade. Not that these possibilities don't continue beyond. But it's a different flavor than the freedom and independence arriving in one's sixties. In the fifties, a special surge of energy and "take no prisoners" attitude came forth. Women spoke of it as a time of reaping; a time to harvest.

There was also a side of counsel about beginning to look ahead wisely. The period between fifty and sixty begins to crystallize the importance of some things and the unimportance of others. This crystallizing begins to prepare us for the rich years ahead, gently launching a thought process about where we might want to live, what relationships we want to invest in, and what thriving might look like over the next few decades. All this happens alongside continued expressing and working—and hopefully alongside increased self-care.

I love what one interviewee said. "Stand for what you bring in your fifties! Don't wait for one more thing to take your seat at the table. Step into yourself fully. If every woman acted and spoke from her essence the world would be so different! We need it. Don't wait 'until.' Do it now."

As I often heard a "go for it" blast of counsel for women in their fifties, I also heard a new and different empowerment that seems to arrive when entering our sixties.

I caught whole new glimpses of the expanded ways women in their sixties and seventies are expressing bursts of new effort and soulful passions in areas that feel deeply satisfying—and that further the evolution of good in the world. Where physical fertility has waned, spiritual fertility and creativity are birthing! Not only did I hear this in abundant measure from women in their sixties, but also the arrival, perhaps slowly, of active assurance that evolution—life itself—has a larger pattern that we've lived long enough to see and trust. The combination of creative energy, conscious un-tethering from things that no longer serve us nor that we want to serve, and trust in a larger design allows us to embody and engage an enlivened, exciting way of being.

Even in the wilderness of the transition, many women in their sixties recognize the strong impulse to continue becoming—with freedom, active wonder, liberation, and a deeper joy that life is living through us. Cultural anthropologist Mary Catherine Bateson calls this the presence of "active wisdom."[1] I call it "active assurance"; a growing awareness of life's patterns and our natural inclination to play an engaged role in them. We realize we are so not done!—and begin to face down the lies of cultural programming that have surrounded us for centuries.

Women in their seventies were also far more engaged across many domains than I realized when I began this interview process—doing things for the first time or acting on long-held desires they've always wanted to express outwardly. It's as if the active assurance and burst of creativity in our sixties takes deeper root in its expression during our seventh decade, each woman's experience unfolding individually in this new stage of life and its new path.

We also seem to be recognizing that we're the product of the women's liberation movement, whether we consciously partici-pated in it or not. It was in our time that we stepped into places of leadership, though a long hard climb for many of us who did. Simultaneously, we raised children, poured our attention into our families and communities, and tried to take care of our-

---

1   Mary Catherine Bateson, *Composing a Further Life: The Age of Active Wisdom* (New York: Alfred A. Knopf, 2010).

selves in the midst of the grand juggle. An interviewee made the profoundly simple statement about "the gems we are bringing forward" as a result. Indeed, the world seems to be calling for what we've learned; what we know.

What great potential to be leaders and guides!

And what an opening to create a new narrative not just for ourselves, but for its promise about everyone.

There is a certain quality to the unique standpoint of women over sixty and the strength that comes with it—a lively embodiment of what it means to break new ground, be playful, be on fire in new ways—and not to be lulled by the cultural expectation that we are slowing down, dulling out, less able.

New ground for women who are well over fifty? Indeed. And not only that, there's a whole new flourishing field of flowers and trees and rivers and valleys and mountains on that new ground. That is what this book is talking about.

At one point in the process of writing this book, I stopped to consider whether I should completely reshape its focus, leave out the interviews with women in their fifties and narrow it to those of us at sixty and beyond who represent the especially notable rising of a new narrative. But I realized several things that I value greatly by including the fifth decade in this conversation—things that I believe are important to readers of this Declaration.

First, responses from women in their fifties and the life patterns of that decade, especially related to work and life priorities, actually help crystallize the decade differences.

Second, the differences I gleaned from one's early fifties to one's late fifties are significant. The shift that begins to happen—especially related to the theme "Done With That"—takes place for many during this decade.

Third, the timing and unfolding of our "Further Becoming" is unique to each woman, so there is nothing set in stone, per se, about decades. They represent general categories of time, not predestined limits or precalculated predictions.

In fact, we refuse to fall for the masculinized form of limited, linear thinking! Rather, the generalizations I make regarding decades as revealed by the responses in the 100 interviews, are to release fears of limitation and celebrate not only what is possible, but what is happening.

The rising. It's here. And we are beginning to claim it.

A DECLARATION OF FURTHER BECOMING

I call this book and its ten key themes a *Declaration* because it proclaims what is here; what is dynamic and active at this moment in time, and how the alchemy of the ten themes is directly linked to Further Becoming. We're seeing it everywhere with women over fifty.

It's also a decidedly feminine blend of wisdom.

One of the ways this wisdom emerged in the 100 interviews was the degree to which women felt this new way of being is a *process* rather than any assertion about an arrival. This is an ode to how women see themselves: on a path—unfolding, emerging, and new—rather than resting in a destination. Such is the way of the feminine.

This is also why the language of the Declaration is: "We are learning…"

No less profound, its pronouncements leave room, always, for more.

Since the word "feminine" is used throughout the book, I offer my definition as a set of qualities available to *all* genders but more associated and perhaps more readily expressed by women. Receptivity, intuition, grace, preservation of life, patient perseverance, the ability to hold complexity, sensitivity to timing, diligence, resolve, humility, and moral fiber—these to me are hallmarks of the feminine. Not as boisterous bravado or a continuation of the feminist fervor once needed and necessary in the past, the *Declaration of Further Becoming* and its model of living and leading from a new place counteracts overuse of the masculine, but does not reject it wholesale.

This kind of living and leading, especially when blended with the best of masculine qualities such as strength, structure, courage, boldness, precision, action, guardianship, etc., allows the best to come forth. Being a woman does not guarantee it, nor does being a man exclude it.

But overuse of the masculine for so many years has warped the well-being of many systems and ways of living, and has led to unhealthiness on a far-reaching scale for organizations, individuals, and whole swaths of humanity.

For these reasons and more, this book is declaring something wholly new.

A GUIDE FOR READING

There are a few details about this Declaration that deserve explanation for easier digestion.

NAMES

In the vast majority of cases, full names of the women I interviewed are used at their initial introduction, then on a first-name basis throughout the rest of the book.

There are a few women who are referred to on a first-name-only basis from the start and remain that way throughout the book. Some of these women requested not having their last names used. Two women who could not be reached for permissions were included as first names only. In the few cases when a woman's story was included but she was not formally interviewed (such as my neighbor) I created a pseudonym. And last, some interviewees created their own pseudonyms so as to preserve their anonymity in cases of sensitive histories or comments.

Every woman's request about how to name and quote her was honored, and the integrity of each story was kept intact. Not every woman interviewed has a story or quote in the book. However, every woman's input, wisdom, and quotes were included in the review and collating of key themes. In that way, every one of the 100 women is reflected in the collective voice of this Declaration.

AGES

Ages noted alongside women's names were at the time of the interview. In some ways it was counterintuitive and almost comical to identify ages at all, since much of the cultural baggage surrounding ages is so limiting and outdated. Innumerable studies point to negative associations made with these numbers, and who wants to perpetuate that?

However, the notation of ages in the context of this book transmits the new narrative: lively voices, strong declarations, active energy, and deeply embodied wisdom borne of juggling so much over so long. These voices and their associated age notations are to emphasize the growing, glowing aliveness of us in our fifties, sixties, seventies, and beyond.

THE MANY NAMES FOR HIGHER POWER

Most of the women I interviewed had spiritual practices and/or a set of spiritual beliefs. These factored in significantly to the way many reflected upon their lives and their priorities.

Different names and languages were used for what would generally be called a Higher Power, the most common examples being Spirit, Source, Love, God, Other, and Divine Other. Some women referred to nature as a reflection of a Higher Power or divinity. Some women used the word Soul, referring either to a Higher Power or to their sense of an individual soul.

I recorded the verbatim words women used for a Higher Power, indicated also in the context within which they were spoken. I capitalized the names that were used in the same way we customarily capitalize the word God, to convey in written form what I heard conveyed verbally.

Of course, there were some women who did not reference any of these words and may not believe in a Higher Power. For this minority, almost all the women still had practices they considered spiritual in some way.

TAKEAWAYS YOU'LL FIND IN EVERY CHAPTER

Each chapter is devoted to one of the Ten Declarations of Further Becoming, altogether representing a new era for women who are well over fifty. I also believe it holds a bundle of truths for younger women!

Every chapter offers the following:

- An overview of each Declaration, explaining what it is and what we are learning about it as we pioneer this new territory.
- Numerous hopeful and helpful examples and quotes from women whose lives highlight each new Declaration.
- At least one in-depth story, allowing readers to meet more deeply some of the interviewees and learn from their footsteps about what's possible.
- A summary section with a series of selected quotes that transmit the crux of each Declaration.
- A statement about what the Declaration is an antidote to—important for us to identify when we're declaring new ground and trying to lift ourselves beyond the false, culturally depressing narrative.
- And finally, simple practices that women everywhere (and men too) can employ if they want to welcome this inspiring life force into their lives more fully.

VOICES OF A NEW NARRATIVE

In these pages you will find stories of women whose lives attest to how stunningly resilient we are—keeping our hearts intact while facing some of the most difficult of human experiences. I also included stories about our natural quest to find spiritual depth and meaning as a lamp for the way to go, especially when we're lost. It is impossible not to be inspired by these women's lives—but more than this, I hope it is impossible not to realize that the truisms they've lived and spoken of are available to us all. The ten themes of the Declaration show us the way.

What I heard in the interviews proved life changing to me. I believe it could be for others, too. I hope the principles and practices in this book help women who may feel stuck or imbalanced in the wilderness period, or who just want to expand into the natural gloriousness of continued becoming.

I do not presume this book and its findings will speak to every woman fifty to seventy-plus. Some women are not looking for a new model nor interested in the energy it takes to explore new territory at this point in life. I completely understand. In fact, I honor where everyone is on her journey of knowing herself.

This Declaration is for the many women well over fifty I've encountered who are almost consumed by the unrest we feel and/or the inexplicable attraction toward a new way of being and living that calls for our attention. This impulse may not reside in us all. But when it's there, it's unmistakable.

May this book affirm, inform, and inspire women everywhere to claim the new narrative that is rising—and to recognize their part in it. May we feel the promise of it and the good it holds for us all, pregnant with possibilities.

OVERVIEW

Exquisite
Being

Pioneer On

Leave Your
Legacy

A Time
for Firsts

Create
a Moai

*A Call To
Further Becoming*

10 New Declarations
from Women
Over 50

Done
With
That

Inhabit
Beauty

Anvil
of Our
Becoming

Tend to
the Vessel

Self-Witnessing
in Solitude

A Call To Further Becoming
10 New Declarations from Women Over 50

Pioneer On
We are learning to continue contributing our gifts to the world in new ways.

A Time for Firsts
We are learning to leap into whole new arenas with creativity and zest—because we want to.

Done With That
We are learning to waste no more time on things that do not serve.

Anvil of Our Becoming
We are learning to value lessons learned from our trials and challenges.

Self-Witnessing in Solitude
We are learning to listen to the quiet within and to a Higher Power, however we define it.

Tend to the Vessel
We are learning to eat well, rest well, exercise well—with love.

Inhabit Beauty
We are learning to be enveloped by the beauty we see and are, within and without.

Create a Moai
We are learning to find sisterhoods where we can be witnessed and celebrated, and witness others.

Leave Your Legacy
We are learning to pass along what we have learned for the evolution and perpetuity of good in the world.

Exquisite Being
We are learning to relish the magic of the ordinary.

PIONEER ON

*We are learning to continue
contributing our gifts to the
world in new ways.*

REFRAMING PIONEERING

I was never attracted to stories about pioneers. Rugged rides over dusty roads, far too much time spent peeling potatoes, soiled clothing and slow stretches filled with meaningless conversation—that's how I pictured a pioneer's life.

I also imagined pioneers as motivated primarily by leaving something behind rather than energized by what was ahead, and of women pioneers doing a lot of the work without much, if any, of the eventual payoff.

No, give me vision and a calling; high-speed jets with touchdowns in new places to be explored and mined for their unique surprises and charms. That's the way I and many of my colleagues lived our professional lives as we juggled work, travel, raising our children, contributing at church, and vacuuming the carpet now and then.

Later, I would learn that the fast track, even while independently running my own company, was still mightily influenced by patriarchal norms of business and production. Like many, I often chose to align with them, unsure there were other choices that could work.

So if anyone told me that a blueprint for Further Becoming over age fifty—and especially beyond sixty—was going to involve pioneering or "soldiering on" in any way, I probably wouldn't be interested. But it's one thing to *choose* to be a pioneer. It's another thing to discover you already *are* one by the very nature of being well over fifty at this moment and carving out a new path, however messy the process, in which to channel your vitality, spiritual learning, and desire to contribute in the world.

That kind of pioneering is what this chapter is about.

The truth is, we are all terribly relevant right now. No wonder we're feeling the call to express our relevance!

"Tell women this is not a time to get into an RV and tour the parks," said one woman I interviewed.

"That narrative about going on cruises or sitting on the porch in repose is not the place of women over sixty anymore," said another. "Don't fall for it!"

It's a far different thing to be encouraged by one's sisters to activate an already-stirring sense of new purpose—laced with the wisdom that doing is not separate from being—than it is to be told to soldier on from the standpoint of masculine messaging.

NOT ABOUT POSITIONS OR RECOGNITION

What came forth in the 100 interviews I conducted reflects a very different standpoint from which we're discerning our unique place as women at this time while contemplating the contributions we want to make. It's a feminine way in the broad sense of the word. It's born of experience and boldly transcends many of the systems we've been swimming in for decades.

On the road of our continued becoming there comes a time when achieving titles or recognized positions is no longer the Holy Grail it once was. But the desire to continue contributing with creativity and well-earned wisdom is still present. Like a flower leaning up toward the light, we too have an urge to continue growing in fresh, perhaps very new, ways.

During that time, I remember having coffee with a friend in her forties, both of us in the midst of reading a wonderful book called *Playing Big* by Tara Mohr. I lauded and applauded the messages in it for my daughter Lilly and my women clients in their thirties and forties. But I remarked how the notion of playing big in the world is not a priority for women over sixty like me anymore, to which she replied, "I can't imagine ever not wanting to play bigger!"

Such is the nub of this profound shift later in life. It's about *quality* more than quantity; the blossoming of new flowers on the tree rather than the extension of its branches. Playing differently vs. playing big.

The measures we use are different, both for the process of achieving what we want, and for the outcome itself. We have less time and tolerance for what the culture trumpets as important or what it says must be sacrificed in order to fulfill a meaningful role in the world. But we still know the impact we can—and do—have.

With personal ego in the back seat, it's easier to see what's truly important to us and how to keep a more fulfilling purpose from this new place.

MY STORY

I personally found this transition disorienting, very nonlinear, and ultimately liberating. I long to say I never felt the looming fear of losing my identity or losing my income stream! But I cannot.

When I was sixty, I was contacted to give a keynote speech at a leadership conference for a global company outside the US. The request had all the usual characteristics: several scoping meetings with senior leaders and the conference organizing team, collecting their goals, sharing my recommendations, reaching into my considerable stash of materials and adding fresh, creative ideas to what I would present, and finding a sidekick to do the work with me. The proposal, the wait, the acceptance. Travel plans. Winter.

This was a dream client in my line of business. In earlier years I would have considered the invitation prized evidence that I'd mastered my craft.

But much of me did not find it fun or learning-filled this time. I'd felt this way before in the last few years, but each time my love for the clients and the Conscious Business content I was delivering were an acceptable enough balance.

And there was also the big question: what would I do if I'm NOT doing this?

To this day I recall driving into Boulder on an errand during the run-up weeks, stopping at the light at Jay Road and Diagonal and looking out at the snowy field to my right. Without necessarily inviting it at that moment, I heard a three-prong message—a mix of intuition all bundled together, accompanied by a deep pit in my stomach. *I think you are done with this, Sue. And I think it's done with you. And, you're not quite ready to hear this yet.*

Indeed I wasn't.

On one hand, something felt complete and satisfied; a sense that my corporate career could not have been better and it might be time to celebrate its completion. But I was so far from done! What does one do with so many years of traveling, teaching, working in complex systems, engaging so closely with people and learning so much from their cultures? And what does one do after so many years of being "in the arena" as Brené Brown terms it?

What does one do when so much of God's, Love's, messages for my life over the years have been woven together in this activity called a career?

The pull of staying with it was strong. I knew this domain so well. This way of being in my career was like a lens through which I saw everything.

As mystery would have it, my mother fell and required intense support shortly before the conference at which I was supposed to deliver the keynote. After clearing it to everyone's satisfaction, I prioritized my mother's care and prepared a colleague to deliver the session.

I was immensely relieved; very telling for someone who has always loved this work!

For nearly two more years, I danced with the seduction to stay full on with my work. Take on a few more clients. Write one or two or four more proposals. Ride the familiar arc. And feel that satisfying sense of purpose along the way. In retrospect, I probably believed that I'd never find as rich a mixture of intriguing activities again.

But there were other influences mixed in, too, that did not feel attractive any longer. Characteristic parts of my career that I'd always engaged with ease felt like a poor use of my time. For example, where international travel still felt agreeable, short in-country travel began to feel onerous. The artificial light in conference centers and training rooms felt oddly foreign to who I was. I even developed a dislike for the plastic mini blinds on so many windows in so many offices around the world.

CONTINUED BECOMING

When we're in the wilderness, we're particularly attuned to "friends" that can help us along the way. My friends were intuition and curiosity, consistently leading me back to my practice of prayer and listening.

Keenly aware that I was approaching closure on my thirty years in this wonderful field, I developed a sense of wonder about this period I was in—well over fifty, still far from elderhood, and feeling tremendous energy and purpose. Nothing like my mother's generation, I looked around for models of what the upcoming decades could look like for women like me. I wasn't interested in traditional retirement—frankly, I didn't even know what that was anymore! What were other women doing? Searching for models—for some body of information about new patterns of life for this stage, I found few.

I started reading and researching. That's when I came across Mary Catherine Bateson, a renowned cultural anthropologist who wrote *Composing a Further Life: The Age of Active Wisdom*.[2] She posits that for the first time in history, we have a new stage of life after adulthood and before elderhood. She calls it Adulthood II. And those of us who are in it right now are pioneering what it means to be living in this stage.

Pioneering!

Bingo!

No wonder this felt like such uncharted territory. Intuitively I knew this was a massive cultural and demographic shift. I've spent my career studying systems and have always been attracted to large-scale change and the possibilities they hold. My curiosity about this felt juicy and life giving.

Bateson's work was a catalyst and a call. She roughly identifies the fifties as the time this new stage begins which influenced my starting point. So inspired by what she terms active wisdom, I was on fire to explore this territory fully. Curiosity abounded.

I love what author Elizabeth Gilbert said. "Curiosity is our friend that teaches us to become ourselves. It's a very gentle friend, very forgiving, and a constant one. Passion is not so constant, not so gentle, not so forgiving—and sometimes not so available."[3]

---

2   Mary Catherine Bateson, *Composing a Further Life: The Age of Active Wisdom* (New York: Alfred A. Knopf, 2010).

3   Elizabeth Gilbert, (2018). "Choosing Curiosity Over Fear" (online). *On Being with Krista Tippett*. May 2018. https://onbeing.org/programs/ elizabeth-gilbert-choosing-curiosity-over-fear-may2018/.

PIONEERING DURING WILDERNESS PERIODS

When intuition and curiosity speak during the wilderness period, they often convey the wisdom neither to move too fast nor get bogged down. Like me, the women I interviewed have learned to rely on their intuition as an important part of direction-setting as they pioneer this new, uncharted phase of life—a very different process than sitting down and fleshing out a linear strategy or approaching a new path from a masculine approach of plan/proceed/achieve.

Not that linear thinking and structured steps don't have their place. They do.

As the stories in this book reflect, women are bringing a blend of masculine and feminine that elevates the best of both and refuses to over-privilege the hyper-masculine so prevalent in our cultural structures and ways of thinking. For women between mid-fifty to seventy-plus who have been in the achievement arena for a long time, they are creating a new Declaration for living and leading, especially during this time of transition.

My own experience reveals that we're not meant to stay in the wilderness forever. Walking with our "friends"—intuition, listening, curiosity, prayer, courage, inspiration, follow-through, experimentation, fearlessness—we can find our way through and into continued becoming that feels purposeful and satisfying, benefiting ourselves and others.

The exact way we arrive at this newly unfolding purpose is as different as we are.

In the 100 life stories I heard—from women with some college education to women with PhDs, women with highly visible corporate careers to women working on the nonprofit front lines, women whose primary focus was raising their families while working part time to women who never had children—I found four themes about the ways we Pioneer On well over age fifty. There were also ten themes about what's important to have in our psychic backpacks as we head into uncharted territory. And a bit of wisdom about how we can get lost if we're not alert.

WHAT PIONEERING ON LOOKS LIKE AFTER FIFTY

1. Birthing the new with continuing threads from the old
2. Freedom and experimentation
3. Continuing the same from a different place
4. Launching "firsts"

WHAT'S IMPORTANT TO CARRY

1. Intuition
2. Acceptance that it can be messy (and that doesn't mean anything's wrong)
3. Self-witnessing: starting with self and our attractions
4. Support/sisterhood
5. Knowing it's not over!
6. Care for the vessel
7. Declaring what we're Done With
8. Considering the legacy we want to leave
9. Valuing how we got to who/where we are
10. Inviting, creating, and surrounding ourselves with beauty along the way

THE TRAIL LEADING NOWHERE: HOW WE GET LOST

1. Inertia/comfort

2. Wanderlust
3. Wonderlost

Again, not all women hear a call to Pioneer On. This is for those who do.

THE ROLE OF INTUITION

The feminine way of Pioneering On gives privilege to intuitive impulses. It recognizes that for a while, while a transition is taking place about one's place and purpose, it may be a mixed bag until the new chosen, or discovered, path becomes clear.

Patience is a hallmark of this process. But it's not the same as waiting for a package of new purpose to arrive with a gift card and bow. It's active. It starts with our awareness that the unfolding of a new or reshaped purpose is as natural as our own continued becoming. After all, who declared that purpose ends at the time a regular paycheck does? Who said it stops when the arc of one particular line of doing comes to an end? This way of thinking, wrapped subtly around what used to be norms of one's corporate or externally structured work life, is more insidious than we think.

Purpose can't ever be taken from us. It might seem to go dormant for a while until we find a way to express it anew. But it doesn't end with a last paycheck or title.

Intuition allows us to be key actors in the shaping of our forward paths. We ask pertinent questions, listen for signs and early whispers of answers, follow through to check out a new idea, and are ready to act when steps can be taken.

Leandra Price is an example. Age seventy-one, Leandra told me how after her divorce she listened to her intuition about what she should do regarding employment, where to live, how to satisfy her desire to be in closer relationship with her daughter. Many things shifted after the divorce, delivering a somewhat unexpected wilderness. Though she loved her job as a college instructor in Colorado, it occurred to her that moving to her daughter's area in Kentucky was attractive. As the two of them spoke about this, one idea led to another.

At the time of my interview with Leandra, she and her daughter had just completed building an addition onto her daughter's home which Leandra said provides "privacy and family—the best of both worlds." She wanted to continue contributing in her fields of mastery: college teaching and mental health. Relying on the same process of intuition, followed by research, and one-step-at-a-time actions, she landed a part-time teaching position at Berea College in Berea, Kentucky, teaching mental health nursing.

"Never in a million years did I expect this," she said.

What a gentle unfolding of a whole new phase of experience at seventy-one! I love Leandra's story and the calm, expectant way she voiced it. It was the voice of active wisdom.

Ellie Sciarra, sixty-one, put it this way. "I've learned that I don't have to 'will it' into the universe. I can, but I'll pay a price for it."

Ellie knows about intuition. Starting as a tap dance artist in her twenties, Ellie tapped and choreographed her way through her thirties and forties with endless energy, making her mark as an outstanding performer and teacher with a growing reputation. But in her fifties, she hit what she describes as a "perfect storm"—menopause, complex health issues, and losing her best friend—resulting in exhaustion she hadn't experienced before. The swirl demanded a lot of letting go and a whole different kind of listening.

"Every day at 5:45 a.m. I walked my dog. That was my time with God/Spirit. It set my day. My task was to listen. I took lots of time by myself that I call meditation moments. I'd go out into nature and feel connected to something greater."

As a result, and even though it caused a temporary identity crisis, Ellie felt the rightness of releasing her roles as a performer and producer. However, she continued to teach dance. Ellie said her greater work was what she considers a spiritual pursuit, helping her let go even more and hear what else might be calling her forward.

"When I was teaching, even in the midst of the continuing storm, I encouraged my students to let go of thinking *their* way, because the exact opposite is what is being called for," she said. "It's in the surrender we find the joy—that's where the tap steps cascade. We let go, let things be, holding the potential for what will come."

Then the studio where she was working raised its rent exponentially, thrusting Ellie again into an urgent question about what she should be doing. She describes the moment she put the whole thing out to Wisdom. "I just said, 'If I'm supposed to teach this class, the universe will show me.'"

Shortly after, Ellie drove by a school—had an impulse to go in—and discovered it contained a beautiful space for rent.

"I'm teaching at that studio now," Ellie said happily at the time of our interview. "But I'm teaching in a different way. I'm not *driving* things or working the same business pipeline, doing all the things you do in the old way. I practice the spirituality I've discovered." She has also choreographed two brilliant new dance pieces and is writing a book. "I feel proud of this work," she said. "It is so demanding and, dare I say, meaningful."

Ellie followed our interview with a quick note about how she's leaning more and more into listening to a voice that is "other than her own" and investing in the important attention this takes.

Sitting with what is not yet clear and asking pertinent questions is worthy work. It's the work of a pioneer.

It is what many wise women (and men) over fifty have learned through hard-earned life lessons. And it's being brought to bear on the transition into and through Adulthood II.

Interviewee Gael McCool, sixty-two, author and transformational coach, said, "I would say to women in their fifties and beyond, listen deeply to yourself in order to follow and trust what emerges. Take the risk and follow it. For some, it's a transition time into becoming our original selves now that a career has been fulfilled and children are grown. Rather than responding to any messages about a need to conform, be deeply original about whoever you're being and whatever you're doing."

"The big difference now," said Veronika Tracy-Smith about her work and life at fifty-two as a marriage and family counselor and co-founder of the online resource Raising Consciousness NOW, "is that I do it all from a different place. It's being pulled instead of driven."

"I honor the guidance that comes through as I listen about what's important," echoed Norma Johnson at sixty-five—poet, performer, and national social justice activist. "It might be about that day, about who I am, what I should be doing. My awareness about just being in a process now is a big thing. Before, I was just "in" it and didn't have the awareness that life has a process. But remembering that I'm not alone and never will be—that I'm participating in creating a world and doing my piece of it—I can trust that."

"If you learn to sit with what doesn't feel good, without trying to force a solution, without an agenda, you learn," said author, editor, and writing coach Molly Walling, age sixty-seven. "Something takes root. There's an intelligence behind this reality we call life. I take it all—my not knowing, my doubts—to the altar. I get replenished and then I can go back to what I was doing until a next step emerges."

In the 100 interviews I conducted, it was remarkable to hear the partnership women have with their intuition. I cover this in-depth in chapter 5 "Self-Witnessing in Solitude." Suffice it to say that it not only provides comfort and assurance, it manifests in tangible ways related to Pioneering On.

BIRTHING THE NEW WITH THREADS FROM THE OLD

In Scotland, Ann Roberts, sixty-four, spent many years devoted to her field of leadership development. Bringing the latest thinking to her work with police officers and other clients, Ann was a picture of what it means to be cutting edge in her field: pursuing certifications, helping managers use effective business principles with their teams, and joining a business academy to remain skilled in her practice.

Ann acknowledged what a time of transition this is for her—but not in the ways she anticipated. Several years ago, Ann began winding down her work in organizational leadership as caretaking for elder parents became more complex. She also felt a growing desire for greater presence in the lives of her adult daughters and grandchildren.

"I began moving away from organizational work—started throwing away books from my office shelves," Ann said. "There was something about letting go…being free of an achievement mindset…and some grief, too."

She carried the threads of her interest in integral theory, management, and coaching with her and slowly began to fuse them with her interest in new topics such as the role of grandparenting. "I see our generation of baby boomers coming into years of intergenerational caring," she said. "It's very new. Look at what we are. I'm not old! I've got these elderly and frail parents, and my daughters have probably thirty more years of me as a mother. My interests are now about me and my family and the community that we are…and how I can bring what I know from my professional work into our family."

In blending the old with the new, Ann decided to pursue a master's degree in applied social research with a focus on wisdom practices, conscious grandparenting, and the flow of love across families. Ann always expected she'd be settled at this point. "But I don't feel settled!" she reported. "It's interesting to be doing an advanced academic degree at age sixty-four. I've got this ambition; this desire!"

People are saying, "Why are you doing this?" and I say, "Because I have to!"

At the time of this writing, Ann and her husband were building an extended family community. Together they've launched a new organization with face-to-face and virtual gatherings focused on intelligent ways to provide intergenerational support where everyone is encouraged to grow. I could hear her edgy desire to bring it all together, unexpectedly pioneering new terrain she didn't foresee.

Ann's story is indicative of much: Winding down work along a specific path. Some sadness in letting go. The unplanned exploration into something new as new circumstances arrived. Channeling pieces of previous professional mastery into a completely different domain.

She never expected to be focusing in these new and different arenas. But an unsuspecting pioneer she has become.

FREEDOM AND EXPERIMENTATION

Newfound energy and bold playfulness emerged for many women I interviewed once they ventured into their fifties and especially when passing the sixty mark. A major part of that freedom was no longer caring what other people think. Liberated from others' opinions and also from cultural norms about what success or acceptability look like at this stage, many women began to experiment with new types of jobs, projects, learning opportunities, and offerings.

This kind of pioneering is full on. Less about visions of a "promised land" and more for the thrill and empowerment of acting on one's unmistakable interests or urges. It can be both the means *and* the end. For me, deciding to interview women was a pioneer's experiment, come what may.

Freedom also comes from the lack of burden about these new

efforts making "sense," or forcing them to relate to a career path or any long-haul commitment.

I loved hearing Marcy Walsh's recent report. Seventy-eight at the time of our interview, Marcy spoke of her marriage of fifty-eight years, raising four children after getting a nontraditional degree in physics and math and later a master's in a whole different field. She had a "volunteer career" as she coined it, including leadership positions at the state and national levels of her church. In her fifties she led hiking trips and European pilgrimages; in her sixties workshops, labyrinth walks, vision quests. Though she loved keeping a house and yard, four months before our interview she and her husband moved into a retirement community where she was still "finding home in a new home" and adjusting to a new space, to no more cooking, to new friends, and even to the relief of no more yard work. "I'm open to doing what moves my heart. I still get to do and be most of what I always could before."

Ever a doer, Marcy felt curious to try something new. "I just led my first retreat on contemplative practices!" she said. Checking in with her two years later, I find her still ensconced in these retreats—and loving them.

Bravo Marcy! How grand to allow ourselves to experiment with something we might want to do and allow ourselves to see if it's a good fit. Like Marcy, we might also reach out for something we didn't know we could do and find satisfaction. And meanwhile, all her participants were delighted!

Experimentation while pioneering is liberating. It honors the importance of our natural attraction to certain activities and the confidence to act on that attraction—something the norms of the past often discouraged for women. Why not listen to our inclinations?

Virginia Macali, sixty-one, started out in government and public service, working in the Ohio Statehouse and other state agencies, and going on to obtain a law degree. After many years managing a staff and continuing to apply expertise in legislative and tax policy, she noticed that "change started happening" within and without. Her friends were leaving the agency and she herself was developing new curiosity about how adults grow and change and about what she termed the connection of mind/body/spirit.

Virginia left her law and government work and pursued a master's in counseling. She eventually was certified as a life coach and established her own coaching practice. This career continued for twenty years.

Once again, in her mid-fifties she began to question what the next phase of work might be for her. What did she want to do next?

"So I started experimenting," she said.

Experiment #1 was becoming trained and certified as an Urban Zen Integrative Therapist. In a clinical setting, she provided yoga and other mind/body practices for patients, caregivers, and staff. Needless to say, this was new territory for her. "I discovered I don't want to work in a clinical setting!" she said. Though Virginia chose to continue her training in nonclinical settings for a while, this was not to be a major career shift. Successful learning!

Experiment #2 was administrative in nature. Virginia accepted an administrative director position with her local PBS station, coordinating their new focus on finding meaning in act three of one's life. She coordinated programs and a popular blog featuring experts on life/work after age fifty, as well as offering her own life and career expertise throughout its administration. The program fulfilled its initial goals, and so did Virginia's second experiment. Another success!

Experiment #3 was to bring expertise from her law background into her new coaching practice using retirement readiness assessments and helping people plan for the next chapter of their lives. "This is the new focus of my business," she said. "My personal and spiritual growth is most important at this stage. It's not important that I do what's culturally acceptable or keep up an appearance of anything. Even doing these experiments—starting and stopping—is a reflection of this.

"There's something that feels celebratory to me about this age!" she continued. "The question is, how can we keep celebrating by doing what we want to do?"

Many of us are drawn to the freedom experimenting allows and no longer the least bit distracted by what anyone might think. Our individual ways of becoming and continuing to evolve are worthy of the spunk, speed, and energy we want to give them.

Tami Simon, fifty-three, CEO of Sounds True, founded her world-renowned multimedia publishing company when she was twenty-two years old. She told me her entire career path has been experimental. Wanting a seat at the table—an avenue through which she could express her passion, her professional desires, and her love of spiritual education—and "desperate to find a way to be alive"—she took one small exploratory step at a time. Slowly enacting the only thing she felt suited to do and animated by that mighty yearning, Sounds True came forth out of confusion, effort, deep prayer, and a continued calling.

Over these thirty-three years, Tami has interviewed many of the world's leading spiritual teachers about their discoveries while navigating their own lives and whatever conditions they have faced. In addition to disseminating wisdom in the form of books and audio programs through Sounds True, she hosts a weekly podcast called *Insights at the Edge* and has authored her own program *Being True: What Matters Most in Work, Life, and Love*.[4] In our interview, Tami encouraged women of any age with these words: "Allow it all to crumble and let emerge all the new things. There may not be a script for you. There may not be a map."

Indeed, we're learning there often isn't.

No matter one's unfolding path in the stage between fifty to seventy-plus, I encourage women to *translate* feelings of bewilderment into an affirmation of freedom. I also encourage translation of the wild uncharted territory of a personal wilderness into an invitation to experiment. Not a Hallmark card dismissal, sugarcoating the challenges at this stage, but a rally cry to remember: *we are pioneering something entirely new*. We as women have never been here before: fully ready to enact a new period of life after breaking through all kinds of barriers up until now. Strong, able, energized, and smart we are.

So where do we start when there is no map?

---

4   Tami Simon, *Being True: What Matters Most in Work, Life, and Love* (Louisville, CO: Sounds True Publishing, 2016).

OUR INTERIOR IS THE STARTING PLACE

Sometimes women have a desire to contribute and an abundance of energy, experience, and skills. But the big "where?" and "what next?" loom large. How does one know the best direction toward which she should Pioneer On?

Without an obvious place or activity calling one's attention, the wisdom I heard in the 100 interviews suggests that the best starting place is one's inner voice speaking to the self.

Rather than identifying *outer* goals and aims, many of the women I spoke with first identify the *inner* world to which they are giving priority. Everything else flows from honoring the true honest desire of what their inner voice is revealing.

At sixty-six, thandiwe Watts-Jones (first name purposefully lower case) is still full on though she used the phrase "newly retired" at the start of our interview. A PhD from Duke, MFA in creative nonfiction, decades as a family therapist and then consultant to educational faculty on racial/social justice issues, Dee (her nickname) has thought a great deal about priorities at this time in her life. As she continues contributing at Ackerman Institute for the Family and finishes a memoir, she reflected on how radical it is to claim our years well beyond age fifty as ones of continued possibilities.

"For me at this stage," she said, "a big priority is fulfillment— seeing the flow of life in general—and finding my place in that lineup. Fertility goes way beyond the ovaries! You can be fertile by finding what it is your mind and heart want to do."

"We all have original medicine as cultural anthropologist Angeles Arrien called it—the main thing we have come here to be," said

Joanna Colbert, artist, writer, and tarot creator/teacher at sixty-four. "It's so important to listen for what that is. I think when we have all these years of experience, we begin to see who we really are and have always been."

Starting with ourselves and recognizing our authentic inner voice leads outward, like a fountainhead ready to emit a fresh flow of water from its deep reservoir. It may show up in writing, mentoring, starting a new business, or changing an existing business culture to become more caring, conscientious, and compassionate.

For some women, this may be very new territory. This is understandable when the daily call of our culture was to become what *it* deemed successful. The process of discovering who one really is—including what we love, what our natural gifts are, how our gifts meet the needs of the world in some way—is a thrilling wilderness for women who may never have had the time, permission, or inclination to navigate it before.

Honoring oneself and being true to one's authenticity is the way of Pioneering On. We are on a journey that has little to do with getting to a particular destination, but has everything to do with how we travel there.

A BLEND OF BEING AND DOING

For some women, continuing right on in one's current career path is what we want to do. There's no reason not to. Women (and men) over fifty, sixty, seventy can bring to their professions new insights, processes, and wisdom borne of experience and seasoning. There can be an ease to this, not felt in earlier decades—the ease that comes from unconscious competence.

What I mean by "unconscious competence" is a deep knowing about how things work, and how to effortlessly advance a next step of progress. It's deeply intuitive; a pattern of recognition and skillful action has sometimes become so embodied we don't know we have it. Women are particularly prone to it, especially the lack of recognition about the presence of our competencies! As we are so aware, our culture has grossly under-lauded the contributions of women, and even more so undervalued women of color.

Annette Thornton, sixty-two, is a marvelous example of hard-earned competence. An associate professor of theatre at a university in Michigan, Annette was in the midst of directing a Greek play. As she coached individual students and directed the arc of the entire performance during regular rehearsals, she attended a virtual women's group I was facilitating over a six-month period focusing on purpose. In the group, we all heard her delight and genuine surprise at how masterfully her students were showing up on stage and radiating confidence and mastery—changing and growing in front of her eyes.

After we listened to her describe this with delighted awe, we mirrored back the direct link between her coaching of the students and the quality of their performance. I remember saying to her in one particular group session, "Annette, I have two words for you: unconscious competence!" The rest of the group built upon this. We saw so clearly what she could not see in herself. She was actually puzzled that it all seemed so easy.

Puzzled!!

Women often underrate the tremendous fruits we've achieved from years of work. The ease of earned mastery puzzles us. Rather than chest-beating about it, we wonder what's wrong.

Nothing is wrong.

Carry on, and enjoy it!

Weeks later, Annette was asked by a regional theatre company to conduct a strategic planning session. By then, she had wind beneath her wings from the encouragement and witnessing of our women's group. "It was unbelievably successful," she said. "I have to say, I was fabulous!"

Indeed she was.

If you love your work, this can be a time to enjoy the competence you have acquired and all that comes with it.

And beware well-meaning questions rooted in old models of thinking while you're doing so, too.

"So, are you retired yet?"

"Are you getting antsy for retirement?"

"So…what are you doing these days?" (As if you're surely not still working!)

At a fundraiser I attended recently, I sat at a table with an immigration lawyer in her mid-sixties. She said to me, "I plan to practice law until the day I die. I love it. We need good lawyers. And now, I get to use new governmental policies to train bilingual legal reps who can't pursue law degrees because of the cost, but can represent incoming immigrants through certification. I'm starting to take a less hands-on approach as they become more skilled. I love the manner in which I can be an attorney now."

And I love how she owned her legal mastery and was doing it in just the way she wanted.

CONTINUING ALONG THE SAME LINES FROM A DIFFERENT PLACE

Sometimes we may need to refresh our approach in order to continue on. It may be similar to the phenomenon of the Great Lakes in the US which actually turn over when a confluence of properties merges together: the surface temperature of the water, the air, and particulars about the thermo cline. We may find we want, or need, a complete turning over of what is familiar in order to "reset" for freshness and continued thriving.

As one interviewee told me, "It's the same priorities in terms of goals, but I approach them with new depth."

Sue Coffee, fifty-seven, considers herself an entrepreneurial artist, and indeed she is. Though she started at St. John's College (known as the "great books school"), she ultimately knew it was music she wanted. Following graduation from St. John's, she headed to Manhattan School of Music and then on to graduate studies at the University of Northern Colorado. Eventually, she joined the Denver Women's Chorus, found she loved it, and saw it as a path to integrate her activism, her lesbian self, and her musical aspirations. Sparking a creative idea to found her own chorus, she did just that using "a strongly feminine model of leadership, but not consensus."

As the founder and director of the nineteen-voice Sound Circle, now in its twenty-second year, and the 125-women Resonance Chorus, now in its fourteenth year, Sue was producing and conducting a full season of concerts each year for both ensembles—each with its own distinct theme, guest musicians, and carefully chosen programming, often featuring new and edgy works. Her choruses have released six CDs. Both groups perform regularly and also provide unique musical contributions at various social justice events such as Hope Lights the Night, a memorial/awareness event for those who have been touched by suicide.

Sue told me how four years ago she felt she'd established a successful path and done good work. She wasn't exactly bored, but it felt stale. She then recalled having read a quote about how boredom often arises before a significant change, as if a new way of being may want to emerge. So she journaled. Had a sense that her body might have some wisdom. Started yoga. Around the same time she began experiencing chronic hip pain. A light bulb went on, she said. She realized she had reached a fork in the road: either she was to take care of the hip and the staleness fully, or it was going to overtake her.

She started working with a personal trainer. Through the process of addressing her hip—but far more by addressing the feeling of stagnation—she hit what she calls "a beginner's mind about it all."

A whole new way of being emerged. She began to address everything from the perspective of a beginner's mind including engrained patterns of thinking. Reaching out for inspiration and guidance, Sue contracted a range of coaching professionals in different domains for support and fresh ideas. She became a beginning cellist and a beginning birder. She began working more assiduously on her own singing voice, worked with a business coach, and established other new routines.

She now begins with morning yoga intermingled with other practices throughout the day. She carves out specific time to think about people in her "inner circle of love" in a focused way—some would call it prayer—in a gratitude/awareness practice. At various times in the day, she sits quietly to study music: hearing it in her head, feeling her way through a potential performance, and "thinking about the people I'm musick-ing with." Other practices, like singing/improvising with a drone, keep her musically fresh. "These are all spiritual practices," Sue said. "In fact, my basic work in the world, through music, is a spiritual practice."

"I feel crisper. Lighter. I've achieved a capacity to lighten up about everything and to focus better. Flow is one of my favorite words."

And the result of creating a beginner's mind about it all?

"My ensembles sound better than ever. My singers say I'm more at ease and more fun. And I've found ways to keep growing that have made me much happier."

Continuing along the same lines from a different place, birthing the new with threads from the old, enacting our freedom to exper- iment, or launching first-time endeavors as covered in chapter 2, "A Time for Firsts," are all ways that women well over fifty are charting fresh territory. Women of past decades had little or no professional standing from which to pioneer this space or build up the skills and cultural currency to establish these bold paths. But we do.

Of course, some women may still choose traditional models of retirement. I didn't capture these in the examples because they don't represent new territory. These familiar paths of the past may still introduce an internal wilderness. Not every woman wants to pioneer anything, nor feels the need to have a map of this territory from mid-fifty to seventy-plus. But for others, retirement itself is being redefined: by *them*.

AND WHAT ABOUT RETIREMENT?

It's a word that doesn't compute for many of us, especially those of us who haven't had traditional jobs with regular pay and pension plans. But "retirement" continues as a catch-all phrase: for not having a regular schedule; not having to be anywhere; not having to produce; not having to answer to anyone.

To some, retirement conveys freedom. To others, it conveys boredom.

To some it sounds like relief. To others is conjures up the end of being part of a community or family—suspended into lack of inbuilt connection.

Some people find that traditional retirement delivers a disorienting lack of purpose and meaning. Others—many women, for example—find it a reprieve where they can move on to things they've long wanted to do.

I overheard a phrase recently that said in essence, "Men retire to relaxation after having enjoyed the privilege and power that comes with their status in society. Women reach retirement age and realize how much access and power has been denied them, and now feel a new surge of energy to express themselves without limitations."

Of course, one cannot necessarily draw firm lines between men and women in this way—it is speaking rather to historical patterns that have been systematized in ways about which men are often unaware. But this dynamic is why the power of Pioneering On is so important to women over fifty if we want to do so.

In terms of hard-earned traditional retirement, I love the way Martie McMane talked about it.

Martie, now seventy-three, worked until age seventy-two as senior pastor of a packed and popular congregation in Colorado with a membership of 800. Her workdays were usually twelve hours. She decided to retire while she still loved it and announced it in such a way that a careful succession plan could be orchestrated. When Rev. McMane exited her lifelong career and role at the Congregational Church, she said, "I fully loved my ministry right up until the day I retired. And the next day, I fully loved my retirement. It was a blessing to be a pastor, and it's a blessing to still be of service—but now in a different way."

Since retiring, Martie has begun a regular physical workout practice—"something I put off for a long time,"—through a combination of NIA (a low-impact dance workout) three times per week and a one-hour class incorporating low-impact aerobics, strength, and balance training in the Silver Sneakers Boom program. She also participates in a restorative yoga class once a week in her home with four other retired women. This physical workout domain of Martie's "retired" life is in addition to creating art and offering small group experiences to help people grow spiritually.

Though some pieces of Martie's retirement may sound traditional, others decidedly do not. Loving her work right up to the last minute, sensing exactly the right time to leave for herself and her organization, swinging immediately into heightened self-care, artistic expression, and continued service to others are all markers of retirement-as-shift rather than retirement-as-end.

Barbara Alexander, sixty-six, has no intentions of retiring as a psychotherapist, coach, and spiritual teacher—but she did apply for automatic healthcare coverage as required by law and after contributing all these working years. "How odd it was to sign up for Medicare at sixty-five," she said. "I'm not old, not retired, have no intention of retiring—but rather am more alive, awake, and full of energy and passion than I've ever been in my life." As she teaches workshops and counsels individuals worldwide, Barbara is a new model indeed for what non-retirement looks like when none of the old norms fit any longer.

Nancy Chapin, sixty-four, who we meet in more detail later, voiced a similar dynamic. When planning her retirement from work as a librarian in a women's prison, she told me that she asked herself over and over, "Is it possible to want to retire from something that you don't dislike? Is that normal to want to retire even though you like what you're doing?" Of course, the answer is yes.

We don't have to dislike, be weary of, or grow despondent in the jobs we've held for many years. We can leave them ("retire") while we still love them if something new is calling!

Dorianne Cotter-Lockard, sixty, and her husband decided to semi-retire somewhat unexpectedly when a business contract she secured fell through and her husband, Jim's work came to a natural end. They sold what they had, decided to travel on a low budget through Europe and maintain a home base with just a few belongings for short periods of time in each place. While her husband continues his writing, she is also writing her first ever books—not one, but two. Both books focus on leadership: the first drawing on her years as a professional musician, and the second, just published, on her years as a business consultant. Amid these activities, Dorianne also reinvented her business, developed a new website with refreshed branding, published a scholarly paper and two chapters in others' books, and completed a project coaching sixty leaders in countries worldwide. (Reminder: this within the definition of "semi-retired"!) Just settling into a new apartment and lifestyle in Lyon, France, Dorianne reports learning French while being required to speak it.

Ah, the ways we are pioneering what retirement looks like!

Janice Character was a pioneer in many ways at ExxonMobil. A woman of color, she grew up in external poverty but never with penury of possibilities. Earning a degree in civil engineering from an Ivy League school, she was hired by Exxon and rose through the ranks from working in sales to marketing, then engineering and on into an executive position. "It was quite remarkable for an African American woman," she said. "It was huge."

Indeed.

In 2014 at age fifty-five, after remarrying a second time and learning that she had four aneurisms, Janice "just got this call" to retire and spend more time tending relationships. "I just decided it was time to go," she said after being expected to be on call all the time in her executive role and not having much time to play. "I gave them two months," she said, "and it was absolutely the right thing for me." At the time of this writing, Janice was just embarking on a trip to Chicago—to run the Chicago Marathon! How's that for staying active after retirement?

Women who have worked in patriarchal organizations, and especially women of color who have had to work exponentially harder to prove themselves, may well look at retirement as a time to flourish in new ways totally outside the structures of many decades.

Yes!

Yes to all the ways our inner sense of knowing knocks on the door of consciousness and invites us to consider what good a change might hold!

GETTING LOST

Recently on a four-hour flight, I sat next to a couple in their mid-sixties. I was busily writing—so much so that the woman next to me asked if I had a deadline. I told her I was writing a book about new tracks women are laying down after fifty during the phase Mary Catherine Bateson calls Adulthood II. I mentioned how uplifting and motivating it's been for me to hear examples of the lively, purposeful ways women are living their lives during what used to be called retirement years.

"Oh," she said. "I retired four years ago. I was senior administrator at a children's adoption agency. We moved back to our hometown and are still trying to figure out what our purpose is now." She pointed to her husband to explain the word 'our.'

What have you been doing these four years? I asked.

"We take long walks," she said, "and we go on road trips sometimes. And we volunteer a half day a week."

Both were fit, educated, and articulate, with solid professional experience. Neither had children. To be honest, one sentence rang out in the back of my mind: *And four years from now we'll be sitting on another plane and you will probably be saying exactly the same thing.*

As I've learned from my years of coaching added to the 100 interviews I conducted—and from my own many mistakes—purpose does not jump out of the woods and announce itself while we're on a walk. How often I've wished that was the case! But it isn't.

Purpose may well not take the form of what *two* people want to do, either. The latter takes a great deal of work to envision, talk about, plan, listen, tweak, talk more, to discern, and create a partnered purpose that reflects each person's unique skills in a way that meets some void in the world.

In other words, we can be unrealistic about how a satisfying journey of Pioneering On might come about.

We might also find it difficult to admit that we may want to coast, especially for a while.

"Travel, relaxation, and tennis are dissatisfying," said Charlotte Tomaino, seventy, who we meet in more detail later. "We need to create a sense of purpose. Aliveness waits there. People may be getting *out*…but that doesn't mean they're getting *in* to anything.'

I love that statement—and how very true it is! Thank you, Charlotte.

As I write this, I recognize my bias: a bias for how valuable our lives are and how needed are our ideas, energy, and contribution. In a world whose evolution is influenced by every thought and action, I cannot help but feel how under-tapped my two seatmates were on that plane as they entered their fifth year of purpose pondering.

This chapter is not meant to be a recipe for what one should do. It's rather a bundle of avenues proven by many of the 100 women I interviewed and by others who are yearning…striving…motivated…who feel an unmistakable urge, like me, to Pioneer On because we want to, and because we feel the evolutionary impulse calling us and other women to use ourselves in a way that furthers good in the world.

For those who feel this, I offer a few warning signs that I noted during the course of the interviews and all the tangential conversations I've had as I continue to collect life stories and snippets about this new stage of life between adulthood and elderhood.

WARNING SIGNS
INERTIA/EASE

There's a tipping point of inertia that seems to slowly build after people retire and become accustomed to schedule-less-ness and the reality of ease and its associated lack of tension. Having had plenty of tension in my life, I am in favor of harmony and balance! What seems to deliver dissatisfaction and aimlessness, however, is when lack of tension—or what I would call creative tension—morphs into personal ease that dissipates one's native motivation to be growing or serving in some way.

Lest I sound judgmental, I had a brief interlude with this phenomenon during part of the summer I was writing this book.

I auditioned on a whim for a play. I did it partly to have fun, and partly to challenge myself to be edgy with something that would demand exercising my performance muscle again. What I didn't expect was that my two roles in the sold-out five performances would disallow me from doing any writing over a five-week period. I was immersed in my characters, the lines I was memorizing, the costume chasing, the rehearsals. When the performances were over, I barely recognized the other planet I had left and had just returned to: the planet of discipline. I loved this book endeavor and its content. But writing is a demand, and it's sometimes tedious. It was also happening while the Colorado sun was shining over the summer mountains and my inflatable kayak sat in my garage.

Two weeks after the play ended, I still couldn't seem to find my way back to writing. Worse than that, I wasn't sure I wanted to. That scared me. I didn't recognize myself in the land of ease. I wondered if it might be good for me to explore this land more fully. I knew, instinctively, that if I did, I would never come back to the book.

There is no right or wrong at such a crossroads. But this felt significant, and I submitted it to prayer and honest reflection. For me, no matter how seductive and comfortable the ease, allowing the days to entice me to do whatever I wanted, I recognized this book was mine to do. The 100 women's voices contained in this book were meant to be heard, and the coalescing of key themes was mine alone to do. Not from an external "should," nor from obligation to the 100 women. But from the intuition I wrote about earlier in this chapter.

I stood at the kitchen sink one day and asked "divine Mind"[5] (a synonym I learned for God or a Higher Power) that I might hear how to reengage the writing in a way that was not painful. (How's that for a prayer?) About ten minutes later, I felt attracted to going back to look at the sequence of chapters I outlined. Not to start writing where I left off, which would have been in linear sequence, but to revisit the overall arc. I did. It was so much fun to re-engage with the arc of the book and allow myself to play with a different order. Then, bingo! I could see that Pioneer On should come first, and Done With That after it, not the other way around. New ideas came about how to make that happen in an inviting way. I practically ran up to my computer to type a new introduction to this chapter.

5   Mary Baker Eddy, *Science and Health with Key to the Scriptures* (Boston, MA: Christian Science Publishing Society, 1875, renewed 1934).

We need not feel shame or self-judgment if ease is attractive for a while. We just want to be alert if it reaches a tipping point where we've decided, through not deciding, to get off any path of Pioneering On.

WANDERLUST

Another confession: I have it.

I'm absolutely convinced that if I didn't have Lilly and Sam, my children-loves, I would have created a life of constant work-travel. I probably would have had a small apartment with no houseplants somewhere—anywhere—because I am so at home on the road. However, having decided to leave a career at Shell in order to establish my own company and be more available as a parent, traditional retirement went out the window. I do not face what one woman called the "tyranny of choice" when it comes to an abundant bank account to travel the world freely, though I'm immensely grateful for what I do have and have earned.

What I noticed during the research—not only the 100 women I interviewed but dozens of others who I did not end up including in this book—is that constant travel for amusement and curiosity *over a long period of time*, and *without a purpose*, is not satisfying. One woman who might appear to most the epitome of retirement's perfect picture with trips abroad every six weeks or so said about her life in a moment of emotional disclosure, "To be honest—I'm lost." Others said this too, from their own experiences and about observations of others in their close networks.

It's not wrong, bad, or immoral. It's just not breaking new ground for future generations to follow, or paving a new path toward the evolution of greater good.

WONDERLOST

The last category of pitfalls I noticed during the wilderness period of this new territory fifty to seventy-plus is what I call Wonderlost.

Taking up personal (inner) spiritual growth and development can be a hugely important priority for women (and men) at any stage of life. But there may well be a point where constantly exploring new teachers (sometimes called gurus), new writings, new discussions—a "seeker" identity—keeps us walking in circles in the zone between what we're leaving behind and what could be forming anew. In other words, a lust for wondering may itself become a pleasant and somewhat lulling wilderness that leads nowhere and, dare I say, benefits no one. When does searching cease to be pioneering of any real sort, inner or outer, and just become a walk around the beautiful woods? I am not sure. But it appears to be something to guard against.

Pioneering On does mean at some point finding and applying what we've learned, in some measure, as we continue our ever-becoming.

HAVING A GUIDING COMPASS

Because we are truly charting new cultural territory at mid-fifties and beyond, we sometimes need a tool to help us orient. Thankfully, we need not adopt or create a tool that will loom over us as a measure of progress or yardstick toward a deadline! In fact, if the notion of Pioneering On was a mandate to continue producing or plodding forward, the interest in having a check-in map might not be interesting at all. Who feels motivated to track our progress when we already know the road contains none of the scenery we love?

However, when Pioneering On is about being engaged in things we love—using who we are and what we know in order to contribute and continue growing in a way that lights us up, then a check-in compass holds a lot more interest. It's not destination oriented, but values oriented. It's not about mile markers but inner markers of meaningful living.

I found in my 100 interviews that the way women kept track of their goals and highest intentions was very individual. Some were more structured than others; some more artistic; some more regular.

Linda Pierce, seventy-one, who we will meet in detail later, keeps track of how she's living using a personal gyroscope—a visual map consisting of six areas: spiritual, physical, financial, intellectual, social, and joyful well-being. "Over time, my priorities shift in these categories," she said, "but the aim is the same: to live a full, diverse life with balance."

Maddisen Krown, fifty-nine, a former learning and development director and now a Holoenergetic® practitioner and management/ executive leadership coach sits each morning in her private space, a hot cup of coffee in hand, and reviews her "Ideal Scene Wheel." In the hub is what she is declaring about herself ("I am…") and around the wheel are five to seven goal areas for the year, similar to Linda's. She sets intentions for the day based upon the goals of her Ideal Scene.

My own check-in process is to return to the set of spiritually oriented intentions and actions I wrote at the start of the year. Once a week, I briefly summarize in mind-map format what I'm accomplishing in each of the categories, emphasizing quality over quantity. I look for progress in some way: for myself, for my relationships, for my work, and for my spiritual growth. If some circles on my map are consistently a bit sparse, I become aware they're domains that need more attention for me to feel happy and balanced. I'm also part of a moai as described further in chapter 7, "Create a Moai"—a group that meets regularly each month and provides support, love, feedback, and accountability about things that matter to each of us, including our life goals.

IT'S NOT OVER!

Traditional models of retirement with markings of bored ease, travel without purpose, volunteering from obligation, or an expectation of decline/uselessness are unattractive to many women at this age and stage. I share this lack of attraction to traditionalism and am all for new ways of living with refreshed purpose. Write the book! Paint the mural and enter exhibits! Teach new classes and retreats. Start the company. Mentor, create, walk in and offer ourselves where we can make a difference. We have no models for this new stage—we ARE the models!

When we find ourselves bumping up against old assumptions and structures, women over fifty are saying internally if not externally, "I'm done with you."

When we feel called to do something new that no one around us seems to understand, we are saying, "Well here I go anyway!"

When we are looking right and left to find role models for how to navigate this new wilderness and clear the way through the thicket, we are often saying, "Looks like I better build my own compass, grab a light of some kind, and make my way forward!"

Our acts of creativity, our acts of movement and health, our acts of resistance, our acts of visibility, our acts of confidence, our acts of spiritual growth, our acts of experimentation, our acts of helping others' development well into our sixties, seventies, eighties, nineties—these are some of the many exciting ways we are breaking new ground. The path of pioneering is a new beginning for generations to come.

QUOTES

"At this time in history we're a new breed of women. We've come out of the women's liberation movement, we've been leaders, we've taken care of ourselves and our families. What gems we are bringing forward! The world is calling for us to be who we authentically are now."

—MARY H., FIFTY-FIVE

"I had everything: a limo, cooking and cleaning done for me, getting invited to important functions. I had to make a choice: money or choosing another path. I took a part-time directorship of an urban mission center with a clothes closet, food pantry, apartment ministry, and a large volunteer staff. I've been doing it for twenty years! I moved into an apartment complex in the city so I could be close to the kids we serve. So many kids have moved in with me for short periods of time. My friends are flying to the south of France in private jets. They wonder why I do what I do. I get up eager every morning. I love working with people! I would say to women: don't ever retire. I'm healthy because of what I do. I'm the happiest I've ever been in my life."

—SCOTTY S., SEVENTY-EIGHT

"I take risks now that I wouldn't have taken before. I take leaps of faith. I have an "I'll figure it out" attitude. It's worth going for everything now."

—CAROL W., SIXTY-ONE

Antidote To

This Declaration is an antidote to the false narrative of already-concluded purpose and society's unconscious assumption about women over fifty, sixty, seventy as useless and invisible. Creative fertility continues! Never about consuming or being consumed, we know our reason for existing is for continued growth, self-expression, and contributing anew in ways as unique as we are.

PRACTICE

Sometimes the pressure to find "purpose" or "new purpose" can feel like a holdover of a parental "should" or masculine models of required productivity.

Let's take the pressure off. Reframe. You're already active: just reading this book means you're contemplating your life. Purpose is something we express rather than find. There are whispers, glimpses, hints arriving all the time about what you might love doing more of or where you're needed.

Have fun considering these questions, making sure not to accept any pressure about how to respond.

- If you were to experiment with one possibility, what experiment would most appeal to you? (Opening a coffee shop? Working with immigrants? Learning to snorkel? Taking a painting class? Studying French cuisine? Embarking on a personal development process? Volunteering with animals? Starting a consulting practice?)
- Who could you talk with to explore this idea?
- What problem, void, or need would this potentially address in

your community, your network of relationships, your church, country, the world, or within yourself?

- What might engaging this activity deliver to you? What's the deeper part of yourself that might get satisfied?
- What small step are you inclined to take right now?

This exercise taps what the feminine may already know: the inner voice providing hints at what brings juice and aliveness to your being. And it is a reminder that your network of resources most likely already includes people and places that can help you with your next step of exploration.

DECLARATION 2

A TIME FOR FIRSTS

We are learning to leap into whole new arenas with creativity and zest—because we want to.

One of the most thrilling outcomes from the interviews was hearing the plethora of "firsts" from women in their fifties, sixties, seventies, eighties. I learned about women becoming stage actresses in their late sixties, picking up new musical instruments in their seventies, becoming competitive athletes on the water at fifty-eight and on the marathon track at sixty-two—and proclaiming whole new roles for themselves publicly—in their seventies ("artist!"), eighties ("author"!), sixties ("CEO!"), and fifties ("traveling photographer!"). Some of them influenced me so profoundly that I followed in their footsteps. (Ask me about the ukulele group class I joined.)

I referred earlier to having felt enlarged by hearing 100 women's stories in general, but in particular, the resounding chorus of firsts completely freed me from any ridiculous assumption or fear-based limitation that hitting a certain age means not taking risks and mastering new things. It truly helps to have role models.

Rosemary, seventy-seven, said this: "Those of us in our seventies, eighties, nineties grew up when women were very limited. We need to accept that we're *limitless*. I'm proud that I was someone who helped pave the way for my daughter who has choices." She continues, "At fifty and sixty, saying yes to your inner voice means wonderful things even if it means giving up what you think is your security. Because you become more authentically who you are. We give that up to become our naked selves. Follow through on that calling—that is something I would advise."

Taking a step to do something for the first time beyond our fifth decade is taking a step toward our own furtherance; an investment in the conviction that we are always still becoming.

It used to be that no one expected women—or men for that matter—to further themselves in creative, business, athletic, or educational endeavors at this stage. After my dad retired from being an elementary school principal with a lifetime in public school administration, he took me out to lunch when I was visiting from college and told me he was considering going back to school for his PhD. I still remember my internal reaction: *What? Why would you do that? I mean, your career is over!* I gave a lukewarm answer at the time, probably to his disappointment, simply not mature enough to see and support how terrific his inclination was.

It never occurred to me that he just wanted to continue learning. That was just like him.

Never too late to reach a new goal or pursue something for interest's sake, we need not be part of any production or achievement cycle to set out on a fun first because it calls to us. My father applied and was accepted anyway, despite my wanting input, and despite very few others doing such at that time.

Further Becoming is always relevant. Expressing our expanding selves in visible ways contributes to an ever-evolving world.

(I hope you're doing exactly that wherever you are, Dad.)

FIRSTS ENERGIZE US AND OTHERS

It may be a small first we enact at the same time we're completing another path. It may also have an unexpected ripple effect.

Anne Weiher, sixty-eight, lost her beloved daughter Liz last year. A retired psychology professor, advocate for mental health and wellness, cancer survivor, and now navigating a Parkinson's diagnosis, Anne might have many reasons to stay home and withdraw. Instead, she signed up for a range of physical workout programs—including spinning! (Spinning is a demanding, full-on-aerobic stationary cycling workout, usually with a barking instructor.)

I saw Anne one day recently after her spinning class. Glowing and radiating pride and happy fatigue, she said, "Wow—the instructor actually came up to me after class and said, 'Anne, you are really working hard.'" She paused. "I must say, I was on cloud nine!"

For one thing, the energy and physical stability spinning helps with has given Anne a more commanding sense of her own life. "Empowering is the word I'd use," she said. It has also helped her deal with her new and demanding puppy, Reeve!

The other thing Anne's spinning did was motivate me to more regular classes at the gym. What excuse could I possibly have, even if writing this book and doing regular yoga, when Anne with less mobility and agility than I have, spins??

We never know what our firsts may inspire in others.

We never know what our foray in a first might deliver to us!

Or perhaps we do—or at least have an intuitive inkling—which is exactly why we make the move.

Pioneers are like that.

CREATIVE ENDEAVORS

One bundle of firsts women spoke of in their interviews was related to creative endeavors: painting, writing, singing, acting, music lessons, gardening.

Sue C. took up the cello at fifty-six.

June took ukulele lessons in her mid-sixties and by her late sixties had joined a ukulele band.

Cindy W. entered her first art exhibition at sixty-one.

Gail, a retired corporate consultant, now seventy-five, is poised to copublish a book containing her professional collage art alongside her partner's poetry. Go Gail!

Marni began learning the Irish whistle at sixty-seven. "I want to keep my brain active!" she said.

At ninety-three, Sandy Hale has performed in two plays already this year. In her late seventies, she completed her first cofounding of a theatre called Viva, part of her newly formed Society for Creative Aging chapter. At eighty, Sandy performed in her first one-woman Fringe Festival show. In her late eighties she started writing a monthly column "Still Truckin" which appears in the *50 Plus Marketplace News* newspaper and for which she still writes—when not traveling internationally, kayaking with her theatre friend, or memorizing lines for her next performance.

Angela Williams, seventy-four, wrote her first book at sixty—and this during a period of time in which she had two brain operations. "I realized that writing a book brought me new energy," she said. "I have so much energy still left." Its second printing has sold out and she has conducted 400 book events over the last three years. "Life is just beginning," she said. "It's not a downhill slide, but freedom!"

Beth Macy, organizational change consultant, dialogue mentor, researcher, and author is writing her first book at seventy-two. She recently had two articles accepted for publication on new research she completed and has just given related presentations at two international conferences in Europe.

Brenda Mehos, fifty-five, exemplifies what leaning into new urges and new learning can do with a whole new set of firsts in her life after her children left home. Still working part time as a hospital pharmacist, Brenda decided to carve out time to take trips with a learning edge to them. She had never been a traveler nor considered herself adventurous. But one trip she was interested in went to the highly charged region of Israel and Palestine. Another trip was a walk on the famous El Camino de Santiago in Spain.

"The trips have been like pilgrimages," she said. "They've been life changing. Travel plus my regular prayer practice are the two things that brought me out of my shell of just a career and kids. Before this I wasn't paying attention to what was going on in the world. Now I've become involved in human rights because of the Israel/Palestine experience. I've talked with peace activists, UN representatives. It has opened up a whole new awareness. I've become an amateur photographer too—with over a thousand photos so far."

There's an unmistakable creative impulse that arrives with playful beckoning to many women once we enter the period of life well over fifty and definitely over sixty. Perhaps we've been so busy taking care of others all these decades, we're finally able to feel this urge and respond to it. And thank goodness we are! The birthing of all kinds of creative endeavors are now becoming part of the cultural landscape for women in the age of active wisdom.

ATHLETIC AND PHYSICAL ENDEAVORS

Move over, old paradigm of slowing, slightly bent women making their way along on shuffling feet. Becoming smaller is no longer the arc of a woman's life! Women are moving happily and rapidly into arenas of physical challenge—because it feels good, builds strength, and reminds us how alive we are. Distractions about falling, failing, or being embarrassed are being replaced with forays into physical fun and challenge.

For example, Marcy skied for the first time in her fifties.

Betsy F. started yoga at sixty-five. In fact, many women started yoga after age sixty!

Martie had put off physical workouts until seventy-three when she retired. Then she started a regular practice of NIA, yoga, and a class mixing balance and aerobics.

I recently met a woman who just took up pole dancing at sixty-one to her own delighted surprise. "I take classes in a supportive all-women's setting where we tune into our unique movements." She lit up when talking about this creative and unexpected adventure she was on. "We don't give a hoot about pleasing the male gaze," she said. "It's such an exhilarating way of moving. I feel joyous, alive, and still sexy in my sixties!"

Katja Stokley, a semi-retired aerospace software engineer, began adaptive rowing classes at age fifty-five and competed in several national rowing regattas at fifty-eight. Diagnosed with MS in her early thirties, Katja also marked her fifty-eighth year by starting to sing in a band and learning to play the clarinet.

Lisa Fisher, fifty-four, managing partner of a property investment firm and lifestyle blogger for "empty nesters" at FeatheredNest.com took her first ever hot-air balloon ride after age fifty, zip-lined through the hill country of Texas and competed in a high ropes course at fifty-three, and joined her first ever axe-throwing league at fifty-four. (Yes. Axe throwing. Where have you been, full life?)

FURTHER EDUCATION

It seems another enticing aspect of our continued becoming is an unquenchable quest for knowledge and learning.

Ann earned her master of science degree in applied social research at sixty-four.

Maddisen finished her PhD in professional coaching and human development at sixty-one.

Karen Metcalfe foresees completing her PhD at sixty-five in benefits of heart-centered leadership.

Rosemary became certified in homeopathy at sixty-five, finished seminary at seventy-one, and became ordained shortly after. She just started a Caring Communities program that is being scaled nationally.

Yolanda Sandoval, fifty-five, an experienced business analyst, educated herself in an additional new career domain when she decided to invest in real estate and "flip houses" while still working full time at fifty-five. She now calls herself a real estate investor in addition to the corporate position she has filled for the last twenty-five-plus years. "Why not?" she asked. "I've been so careful and frugal all my life. I realize I can go for things now."

Ten or so of my women interviewees had enrolled in writing courses, writing groups, or had hired writing coaches en route to publishing their first books. Their educational pursuits toward the end goal of successful publishing led them to research the publishing industry, mechanisms for self-publishing, and online programs for cover designs. One woman at age sixty learned about and set up her own sound studio in a corner of her home to record her book into audio format.

A woman from a local catering business, who was helping me plan nutritious meals for a women's retreat I was holding, told me she has just earned Certified Nutrition Specialist (CNS) status at sixty-three following a rigorous multiyear study program.

Interestingly, that same week, I was at a holiday gathering and met a woman in her late fifties who had also just completed a nutritionist certificate after mandatory retirement from her air traffic controller career.

BUSINESS LAUNCHES

It was interesting to hear how many women in their sixties proclaimed the arrival of un-tethered entrepreneurial freedom. There seems to be a feeling of emerging sovereignty—true in my own life too—from societal expectations, patriarchal pressure, family responsibilities (for the most part), and the need to ascend any ladder except the ones leaning on our homes when we need to clean the gutters!

While the ground is being paved for this in our fifth decade, it takes a different shift when entering the sixth. With such sovereignty comes whole new vistas. Why not strike out for the first time toward just the spot on the horizon that beckons us?

Marta Turnbull is a wonderful example of striking out anew after sixty.

Marta spent a lifetime working in tech and science labs. As a stable income provider for her family, she carried the responsibility of finances and therefore career progression, gaining expertise in a male-dominated field, and working her way up to project manager of large projects. "For years, I woke up every morning to support my family," Marta recalled.

But Marta knew there was a glass ceiling in the laboratory where she worked. "So through the years, my coworker (and now business partner) and I used to cast about, discussing what to do next, what we wanted to create."

"I've always loved travel," she said. Which is why at age sixty-five, Marta decided to launch an International Women's Travel Center with her coworker. Their mission? Encourage women to travel safely and well. And travel in a way that benefits women in the countries you visit.

"A lot of times we're told we can't or shouldn't do something. Don't let someone else tell you who you are or what you should do! If you have a desire to go solo in the desert—go! Define what you want to do, then go do it. I love images of women riding bikes, rock climbing, writing books!"

Marta said she encourages women to "Start your own business. Provide services and products that really matter. When we work for someone else, especially large male-run companies, it's their priorities. Especially for younger women, being in business for ourselves is how we're going to thrive.

"We are absent in the news and in history, so it's important for women to be generating content," Marta continued. "This is about women not being displayed as objects or models of fashion and lipstick, but presenting ourselves as who we are…doing what we want to do."

Marta also encourages women to be "present, vocal, and making art. Do what you want to do. Do it out loud!"

Marta's bold foray into something new represents the sparkling promise of not only new territory to pioneer in our sixties but the expectation of its continuation if we so choose. Starting a travel business is not nailing together a lemonade stand to come down when the weather changes! It's built to continue.

I discovered women in their sixties expressing liberation to untie from the past and—with enthusiastic animation perhaps as never before—pursue whatever they wanted. Many of the women I interviewed in their sixties were creatively restless and lit up with an adventurous spirit, fully intending to channel their resources of energy, skills, time, and desire. "I can absolutely say: the sixties rock," Marta said.

FULFILLING PASSIONS WITH FIRSTS

In our call to Further Become, any part of ourselves that yearns to be coaxed into fuller expression is worthy of tending.

Allowing first-ever forays into territory we've not yet explored is an expression of the full-on "go for it" of our fifties, the sovereignty of our sixties, and the continued creative urges we still feel in our seventies and eighties.

Deborah Ridley-Kern, fifty-eight, is a longtime educator who knew when her daughter was three years old that she wanted to be a teacher. Starting off as a ballerina, then teaching ballet, starting a family, care-taking her parents while attending school, she earned her education degree over a seven-year period. Steeped in wisdom that comes from perseverance and striving to bring out the best in others, Deborah said, "I wouldn't have women ask themselves what they want to do. They should ask, 'What do I want to learn? What am I eager to know? How do I want to create family and society and the rest of my life with openness and childlikeness?' Everything is possible at this stage."

"Is everything *really* still possible?" we may ask. Or put another way, is learning still available and ripe for the picking no matter our backgrounds? Whether we've planted ourselves in a new place, are low on friends, low on funds, or low on hope that creative fertility really can (and does) still continue?

Many of my interviewees in their seventies would say with gentleness and authority (and a bit of a chuckle), "Why would you even ask?"

I met seventy-year-old Air Force Colonel Lynn Heckler during my interview process of 100 women. That's right—*Colonel* Heckler.

Sixty-nine at the time of our interview, Lynn showed up to our conversation with expectancy and spirit. "This is a privilege," she said, making me want to talk with her all the more!

Lynn went to nursing school in Springfield, Massachusetts. She described it as a perfect fit; a field of study suited for exactly who she was. While there, she met several nurses in the Air Force Reserves who had taken care of war victims in the Philippines. Compelled to apply to the Air Force one morning, Lynn found herself not only accepted quickly but shipped to Thailand in the first year to care for Vietnam War casualties. This was in the 1970s—during which time she shockingly experienced the warfront of a personal kind—that of becoming a battered wife. The demands of her work while navigating the dynamics at home required savvy, perseverance, faith, and needless to say, resilience. Lynn transitioned to the Air Force Reserves for a time and lived temporarily at a battered women's shelter. During this time, she continued to pursue a master's degree in nursing.

"All I can say," Lynn reported, "is when I was facing my dissertation and graduation, everything felt calm. Though he had abused me again, I felt carried by my faith through the whole experience."

Lynn divorced her husband at age thirty-one and went back to active duty in the Air Force, earning the rank of Colonel in 1995 when she was forty-seven years old. When Lynn officially retired from the Air Force four years later at age fifty-one, she intended to do active volunteer work in her soon-to-be new location in Texas.

By then she was happily remarried. At the time, Lynn never expected volunteering for the Council of Women's Ministry Program would bring her face-to-face with so many women who had been abused by their husbands but were still dependent upon them for survival. She could relate. One thing led to the next as Lynn, then fifty-five, listened for a role she could play to support these women equipping themselves to get up and out of the abusive situations.

"I've always loved lifelong learning," she said. "What is our attitude about new experiences? New learning? New ways to organize our lives? *We are not our prior jobs!*" When she was introduced to the Christian Women's Job Corp with life and job-skills training for people in need, Lynn saw the role she might play in bringing the same program and structure to Boerne, Texas where she lived.

"That was thirteen years ago. I've been the executive director ever since." She added, "I jump out of bed every morning!"

Lynn concluded by saying, "We can get to the essence of who we are at any age. We are equally gifted to do new ventures."

What a model Lynn is for this liberating principle! Gifted for new ventures. Yes!

Hats off to you, Colonel Heckler.

Firsts can change our lives and the lives of others—for the better. What better time to act on them than during the age of active wisdom when we're more attuned to what we really want to do?

The liberty to enact our first anything—as long as it's the pull of attraction rather than the push of an expectation—is ours. And why not?

Said Carol K., seventy, "Approach this time as if everyone on the sidelines is cheering you on."

Because we are.

Unmistakably, the overall sentiment from the 100 women to other women at this stage of life is: This is a fertile time with great freedom. We have choices and energy to give things a try, and no reason not to. We deserve it. Follow the muse. Don't hold back. Go for your first!

Story

"What I did at age sixty-seven was more than a little dangerous," said Debbie Anthony, speaking from her new location in Southern China in our Skype interview with seventeen hours' time difference between us. It may have been indeed. But from the sound of Debbie's voice, I heard gleefulness, energy, and edgy excitement about telling me how she got there.

A single mother to three children, Debbie spent much of her thought-energy on how she was going to pay the bills and cover her children's needs. A private school teacher in Texas for twenty-five years, she had always believed she had to take care of herself in whatever ways were required. She had dreams in the back of her mind of going into the world to teach children how to read, but practical daily demands disallowed any serious consideration of it. Like many women I have met in the 100 interviews, Debbie was what I call a warrior mother—rising to whatever the demands, working long hours, striving to challenge herself and contribute at work, church, home, and in between.

"Because I've divorced twice, my life was a war zone at times," she said. But Debbie did not dwell there. "We can easily feel marked out—like marks are made against us," she said. "But all the difficulties actually prepared me."

When her children were older and her private school teaching no longer the right fit, Debbie changed careers and took a management position at a well-known US drugstore chain. "I hated it," she said. But the necessity of continuing to earn income was a pressing demand. Ever a learner, Debbie made a conscious decision to plunge into a deep inventory about herself: what her strengths and talents were, work environments she naturally oriented to, what she truly wanted to do when revisiting her dreams and intuition. Not unlike Sue Coffee's uptake of a "beginner's mind" described in the "Pioneering On" chapter, Debbie completed various assessments, sought out career coaching, and had a regular practice of prayer and listening for guidance.

"There is so much value in knowing yourself—in doing a 360 and valuing who you are," she remarked. "And to do this at every age!"

As she trusted her Self-Witnessing process and her quest for what was next, she was fired from her managerial position. "What a blessing!" she said with a laugh.

After taking time, a deep breath, and collecting unemployment, she decided to move to South Carolina to connect with a ministry specifically for those over age fifty. Reflecting about this age group, Debbie remarked, "In the US, the mindset is: you can retire now. But the fifties is the time in your life you've been preparing for! All the rest is leading up to these years—to have an eternal effect on the earth. To be all you were created to be!" She noticed a mindset of decline descending almost imperceptibly on the groups with whom she worked, and in her view, it wasn't good. "We cannot allow for society to say, 'You're done.'"

One day, when Debbie was sixty-seven years old, she heard someone at the ministry say how much there was a need for English teachers in China. "I just shook my own adventurous hand," she recalled with a song in her voice. "The whole idea from early on was like a diamond in my belly."

I could hear the diamond radiating from Debbie in her voice, her zest, her playfulness, and her joy. It was magnetic to me as I conducted the interview. When she mentioned that her move to

Southern China to teach English to young adults was "more than a little dangerous," I also heard the adventurer in her—the voice of someone who would not have missed it for the world. In fact, she was there because of the call of the world. The office in which I was sitting seemed to expand with Debbie's testament to this first at age sixty-seven—a first that reminds us all of what is possible.

"Way too much emphasis is placed on age," she said. "It's just a number! Neither youth nor age is good nor bad. It's just a *mindset*."

In Debbie's follow-up email to me, I noticed her salutation.

Living the dream, it said. Signed Debbie Anthony.

May every woman in her fifties, sixties, seventies, eighties find and act on whatever first is the waiting diamond in her belly.

QUOTES

"Don't let fear stop you from doing whatever you want right now. It's never too late."

—BETSY M., SIXTY-EIGHT

"For the first time in my life, I have the courage to declare myself an artist."

—GAIL H., SEVENTY-FIVE

"Why not do something entirely new? I've been so careful and frugal all my life. I realize I can go for things now."

—YOLANDA, FIFTY-FIVE

Antidote To

This Declaration puts to rest forever the assumption that new ways of creating, forays into adventurous activities, or reinventing ourselves are for decades past. A whole new blueprint is writing itself as women break new ground and burst forth with declarative action that life is to be explored fully and lived colorfully at this stage too.

PRACTICE

First of all, relax.

This is going to be fun.

With all the myths surrounding this stage of life, we are already playing in the sandbox of new realities. Remember, the days are over of going silent and small into autumn, so to speak.

This practice is about a first...but it's going to flow from a second, or third, or fourth, or millionth. Because there's probably something you've wanted to do for a long time. You've gone there in your mind. Over and over. THAT's the first for you to put into action now.

Ask yourself, how often have you:

- Reached for a paintbrush?
- Picked up a camera to begin shooting that gorgeous scenery?
- Begun to write the book that is in you. (You already know what it's about.)
- Sketched dresses you long to design?

- Fantasized about zip-lining through a green jungle?
- Started training for a marathon while sitting on your couch. Or simply laced up your shoes and headed to the trail nearby to take long brisk walks finally?
- Happily salsa danced in your mind while falling asleep at night?
- Wanted to drum on an African djembe?
- Imagined starting a business doing that thing you've always wanted to do?
- Thought about opening an Airbnb?
- Decorated others' living rooms in your mind—(without telling them, of course)?
- Offered "help" to someone because it's what you love to do: Baking? Help planning an international trip? Translating a document written in another language? Going through a house and getting it ready for sale?
- Begun collecting seashells and wanted to seriously continue?
- Looked at a plane flying overhead and imagined yourself on it, heading finally to the safari or humanitarian aid project?
- Thought about joining a choir?
- Imagined writing music?
- Envisioned opening a small music store?
- Looked at the painting you completed (that your friends love) and thought about entering it in an exhibit?
- Dreamed of sitting in a chair by the water with those spiritual books you want to study?
- Started building something in your mind with your own hands: a barn, a garage, a shed, a gazebo, a new home?
- Heard the hot-air balloon in that colorful valley call to you, even in the off-season?
- Pictured the flower garden you want to plant?

What have you picked up with your hands, or created in joyful abandon, or run toward in your mind? You know what it is.

Now, say it out loud to someone.

Then ask yourself this question: *what small step can I take toward that first?*

Make it a small step. (We've had enough of the big "should" stuff.) If it feels fun…energy producing…heart-poundingly attractive… then move right toward that first step of your first.

And email me to let me know what you've done (sue@bright-mangloverint.com).

DONE WITH THAT

We are learning to waste no more time on things that do not serve.

A fascinating theme emerged unexpectedly as I listened to women tell me their current priorities and what I'll call their desired "use of self" at this time in their lives. "Use of self" is a phrase I was introduced to in my sociology studies in the seventies. I've heard it many times since, usually in the helping professions of social work, therapy, teaching, facilitation. It's basically choosing the best application of one's focus, time, and proactive efforts on behalf of another—but in this case, on behalf of oneself.

Though not every woman I interviewed knew exactly how she wanted to continue growing and contributing, most women resoundingly knew what they were Done With!

CARING WHAT OTHER PEOPLE THINK

When I asked the question, *"What's not important that used to be?"* the most common response was voiced in four oft-repeated words: What other people think. In fact, "Done With" caring about pleasing others, or being concerned about what others might think, was a lively and immediate declaration almost 100 percent across the board. The freedom and confidence associated with no longer caring about others' opinions unleashes all kinds of choices, most notably about how we prioritize our time, choices we make for new projects or work, how we dress, who we spend time with, and where we live.

In other words, a new sense of ownership arrives.

Olivia Parr-Rud, sixty-five, fully realized that her transition from the highly respected male work domain of data mining/data management to the role of consultant about love as an important characteristic of leadership might sound—well—light. Given her considerable prowess as a three-time author—one book on data mining, one on business intelligence, and one on SAS analytics—her foray into compassion and caring as part of a healthy workplace did not align with the cultural respect we typically have for the domains of technology and statistics in which Olivia has a master's degree.

But Olivia is done worrying about whether other people approve of her passion for bringing more love into leadership. In fact, she recently authored a new book titled *Love@Work*. How's that for declaring what she's done with—and pioneering a new path?

EGO RECOGNITION

Closely associated to being Done With any concern about what others think is moving beyond the need for what one interviewee called "ego recognition." We touched upon this in "Pioneering

On"—the disinterest in achieving "titles, public positions, or reaching certain social standards." There is a letting go somewhere beyond age fifty and definitely beyond sixty of this bundle of imposed distractions. Sometimes it happens by choice, and sometimes it's a surprising discovery that the external measures we once considered success symbols no longer represent the Everest we care to climb.

"Earlier, part of me wanted to be a star—really wanted to produce a Broadway show," said the dance teacher Ellie, age sixty-one, whose story is mentioned in chapter 1, "but that doesn't matter now."

Gillian, age sixty, was not a formal participant in the interview process, but a woman I met along the way. She once had a high-powered career as a technology consultant and recalled when "My colleagues at a prestigious firm rang me to ask if I'd like to come onto a big project. I said, 'No, I'm no longer doing that work,'" Gillian told me from her home in the UK. "I told them I'm in the process of opening a bed and breakfast. They were stunned. I heard from one afterwards that they talked among themselves about how they couldn't believe it. I must say, I had a good chuckle. You know when you've turned that corner."

Coming to terms with what we're Done With is crucial to opening up new space for a new way of living, working, being. Whether it's by discovery, decision, or a combination of both, recognizing it is freeing.

STUFF!

I had flip charts on my office wall for six months with data from the 100 interviews. One was a prominent chart with categories of Done With That responses and their corresponding quotes. I laughed many times at one of them, written in green marker and screaming at me from the wall as I cleaned out my office closet and file drawers—adding things to the growing "donate" pile in the hall.

"STUFF," it said.

Oh my, but are we ever Done With storing, looking at, cleaning, rearranging, interacting with, and buying stuff!

"I went through my house and just started giving things away," said Nancy, sixty-four. "I didn't even want to sell them. I just wanted them gone."

Carol W., sixty-one, said, "I live now in two rented rooms—one in Iowa and one in North Carolina. I travel between them to be with family members. I realize I don't need much anymore."

"I no longer buy things for my apartment," said Zoe Freeman at seventy-three. "I don't redecorate anymore—it's not important."

It is significant to note that Zoe is going strong in her full-time job as manager of wellness engagement at Pike Market Senior Center in Seattle. A fan of classical concerts, active in her free time with friends of all ages, applying creative new ideas at work, regular spiritual practices that keep her grounded, energetic, and growing—this is a woman who is full on in her seventh decade.

"I hear about ageism," Zoe said, "and I just won't let that happen to me. Women who say they aren't waited on at a store because they're invisible…that's not going to happen to me. I speak up! And I don't talk about the way things used to be or the things young people do with technology that I can't do. I can learn it."

The point: Zoe's non-investment in redecorating isn't because the arc of her life is diminishing. It's because she's too busy to care about it as a priority anymore!

In my own case, I can almost feel when my closets have too much stuff in them, even with the doors closed. Or maybe it's because I know what's in there! The density of it weighs on me. I want them cleaned out, made spacious. I can think better and move faster that way. It's as if the canvas of my thinking is clearer when the space around me is—and the space behind the closet doors, too.

For many women well over fifty, our stuff represents ways of *thinking* we're Done With. Whether it's fear, pride, unnecessary attachments, we know better than to keep hanging on.

I love the process Beth, seventy at the time of our interview, used for downsizing her belongings. Following a move to a smaller home, Beth created a ritual for getting rid of things. Not wanting to store them further, she felt a need for an honorable way to dispose of memory-laden items—particularly photographs, letters, clippings. At night in her back yard after the neighbors had gone to bed, she took piles of these historical keepsakes, said a prayer of thanks for what each represented, and placed them in the fire-burning grill. She imagined "releasing the memory and any remaining emotions" that might keep her attached to the person or the memory. The day after this tender process, Beth dumped the ashes onto her rose bushes "in hopes that the remains of the memories would help grow something new and beautiful."

DRAINING/EMPTY RELATIONSHIPS

A friend once offered a useful comparison between two types of relationships based on two physics-based energies: endothermic and exothermic. Many women over fifty, it turns out, are Done With endothermic relationships.

Endothermic relationships are when the relational mix (two people or a social group) weakens the involved parties and/or wastes their time and energy, both of which are at a premium in the age of active wisdom. The attention these relationships demand has a net effect of deflecting from the health, happiness, betterment, and growth of those involved, even when experienced occasionally. They suck energy from noble activities one or more parties might otherwise be creating/enjoying.

Exothermic relationships are ones where each person brings his/her whole best self to the mix, and the energy created by the relationship benefits both/all and contributes to the environment around them. The overall effect is enlivening and life-giving.

The 100 women I interviewed mentioned relationships in general as one of the most important things in their lives at this stage of life's journey over fifty—especially once in their late fifties—tied with internal development. So, the contours and content of desirable vs. undesirable relationships becomes critically important. Distinguishing types of relationships we are Done With allows greater clarity about relationships we value and seek to maintain as a contributor to our life satisfaction.

Sometimes *we* may be the one who begins to recognize that a certain social group or relationship is no longer exothermic for our Further Becoming. Others in the group or partnership may still be satisfied with the relational dynamics, including the usual conversational exchanges and how time is spent together. There may be an imbalance in how the relationship is experienced, depending on how each person is continuing to grow and change.

The 100 women I interviewed made reference many times to relationships and types of social activities about which they no longer care to engage. Needless to say, they are all endothermic.

"I say no to many social invitations now," said one woman in her late sixties. "I prefer my own company to superficial socializing. I just cannot abide it anymore."

"Vapid conversation!" said another at fifty-six, representing a large majority of interviewees who used slightly different words.

"Topical conversation. Rapid-rate chatter," said a third who just celebrated her seventieth birthday.

"Getting together, talking over each other, very little listening about anything of substance, and then heading home," said a fourth in her mid-fifties. "When I get home I think, 'what was that?' Why do I keep going?"

A woman in her sixties with whom I shared some of the findings of this research said, "I can relate. I refuse to be around people doing the 'organ recital' thing; what's wrong with this organ, what the specialist said about that organ."

IDENTIFYING AS BEING INCOMPLETE WITHOUT A PARTNER

An area I discovered when interviewing single women specifically was the cessation of any pull toward prioritizing seeking a committed relationship.

Where time and energy were expended on thinking about, seeking, and dating in prior decades, many single women interviewees voiced the same five words about it at this time in life: *if it happens, it happens.*

Put another way, if one's consciousness is a mansion with many rooms, and each room is saved for activities of priority, many single women well over fifty don't have a room labeled "Seeking a Relationship" or "Needing to Be in a Relationship to Feel Complete." I was surprised to learn in the 100 interviews how infrequently finding a life partner came up.

As one of the top two answers to the question "What's most important in your life right now?" women's elaboration on "relationships" meant the wide tent of one's existing family (children, grandchildren, spouse/partner) and close friends...but did not include, for single women, seeking a relationship.

At a talk I gave to a group of twenty women, this same point emerged. The group had a mix of married and single women, gay and heterosexual. After sharing some of the top-line themes of the 100 interviews, a very attractive woman in her sixties raised her hand. "I don't know whether this is strange or not," she said, "but I find at this age I don't care at all about being in a relationship. I have friends and lots of things to do. Is that weird?" She was yoga-esque—slender, fit, a beautiful countenance, and dressed stylishly. In other words, this is a woman who would not have trouble attracting dates if she made herself available for it. She, like many of the women I interviewed, is just not prone to prioritize it.

This is not to say that coldness or sarcastic rejection had emerged out of hopelessness or negativity. Rather, these women recognized a sense of completeness about themselves without being in a marriage or a primary relationship of any kind other than with themselves, their lives, and often their relationship to life itself.

And clearly, they are Done With ever entering partnerships where they would end up "doing the heavy lifting" as one woman in her sixties put it—taking on the emotional work for two or the bulk of daily tasks on behalf of the pair.

"One thing that's not important that used to be is that I no longer need an object to love," said Wendy Appel at fifty-seven. "It's a bit disorienting because it's new. But it feels very freeing."

"I have a sense that God wants me all for Himself or Herself," said Hanitra, in her early fifties. "It is a sense of total freedom."

Said a third in her mid-fifties, who preferred not to be identified by name, "I'm free from the need to be in a relationship, without being indifferent."

"I'm not interested in the investment it takes to date—or whatever you call it at this age," said Marnia, fifty-seven. "I can't explain it, but it's just not important." An entrepreneur pursuing two different types of businesses, she travels, teaches, keeps a home, and is involved in social justice issues as well as being a vigorous jogger and stand-up paddle boarder.

I heard this message in a positive way for both men and women at this stage. To be relieved of the notion that we are somehow made complete with the arrival of another person in our lives weds us also to the correlating belief that we are not complete unless. How silly! Any of us who have lived full lives for five, six, seven decades or more know full well how life and its capacity for wonder, newness, growth, and love are not bounded by prerequisites of two. We are Done With any cultural messaging—perhaps projected for its own uses—that we are "less than" when fully ourselves. We know better.

Some women in my 100 interviews shared that they were currently in the process of deciding whether they would continue in their marriages, often citing lack of mutual growth as the reason for consideration. Many had gone through divorce already, whether in the distant past or recent to the interview. Some had found new life partners after fifty and described their commitment to those marriages as priorities. This "finding" of a new partner occurred naturally and often to their surprise, such as reconnecting with an old high school friend at a thirtieth reunion (twice mentioned in my interviews!) and recognizing both a historical bond and shared affinities that could lead to a happy and balanced marriage. Others spoke of making the marriages they've been in for a long time a high priority. It was a mix.

Of course, the 100 women *did* discuss the kinds of relationships that feed them; the ones we're choosing to stay in or initiating. They're exothermic, for sure. Belonging to an intentional circle of women, such as a "moai" (which is discussed in more detail in chapter 8, "Create a Moai"), fills a very important piece of the relationship picture.

And it seems that for some of us, a new life partner may not come in the form of a person, but in the form of a *purpose*.

The overarching emphasis—whether social groups, individual friendships, family, and/or marriage partners—is that women well over fifty are Done With spending time in social situations/relationships where the main fuel of the relationship isn't exothermic, benefitting everyone's best self. The PS seems to be: *I've got too much I want to do…and time is precious.*

SHOUTING AT WALLS THAT DON'T HEAR OUR VOICES

Caring what other people think, achieving public notoriety, buying/keeping stuff, and participating in endothermic relationships all have the property of releasing that which no longer serves us. The releasing delivers room for new priorities and new ways of being. But this Done With That theme—shouting at brick walls—has a different energy to it. If brick walls represent symbols that used to be fixed forces, either chosen by us, culturally imposed, or both, then being Done With them is a significant pronouncement about how we're shifting our focus, energy, finances, and time.

And time, energy, finances, and focus are powerful resources for any demographic group to shift.

This Done With That theme has an activist edge to it. It's work related, but less about types of *professions* than types of *environments*. Specifically, we are Done With:

Environments that do not welcome our views.

Environments that are so production oriented that the human conditions within which we're producing aren't conducive to the full use of our skills, intellect, and heart.

If there's a catch-all word for the environments women are Done With, it's *patriarchal*. The word patriarchal might seem to suggest these are always environments where men are in senior positions. Indeed, the history of corporations in most countries certainly confirms male seniority in positions, pay, and influence. But some companies whose values include healthy, conscious, values-based work environments are also led by men.

The environments we are Done With are those whose characteristics are excluding and top-centric rather than honoring the input and work of women and people of color in addition to men—therefore informally or formally keeping the status quo in place.

In my own case, I had the privilege of working in one of the world's largest oil and gas companies in a senior global consulting role. Its history is certainly of white men in senior positions. I was privy to every part of what was wonderful, growth stimulating, exciting and accelerating to one's career by working there. Women were slowly being promoted into more senior roles though they had to work twice as hard to be seen, valued, and moved up. Two of the female managers in that company were the most important mentors in my life. I also was privy to what concentrated power in the hands of a nondiverse small team at the top of a steep hierarchy looks like and can do, the voting power of which impacts literally millions of lives across the developing and developed world. I would not have missed the learning and opportunities for anything, and am immensely grateful for what it brought into my life. I'm also aware of the shadow side to any company and the tremendous power it wields.

Before founding my own company, I was also hired for a short time by a women-run organization with a fine reputation and a good expression of diversity in terms of its managers and staff. Despite its reputation as a values-based organization, I experienced working conditions, even at senior levels like mine, as overly production-oriented, almost assembly-line-like with a mandate that we should remain focused solely on our tasks and not on building relationships with one another.

Anyone with a modicum of active wisdom knows that worthwhile outcomes are achieved at least partly through relationships and connection; the product of a system of collaboration. We are not machines, nor do we want to be. The environment was anything but respectful of balance, courtesy, collaboration. I left after six months and can echo what many women are saying: an overfocus on production for the achievement of profit, without regard to the conditions of producing, is something we are Done With, whether led by women or men.

I appreciate how Cindy Wigglesworth, sixty, talked about this topic in our interview.

After a twenty-year career at ExxonMobil, Cindy delved into a decade of research on developmental intelligence and spiritual wisdom captured in her book *SQ21: The Twenty-One Skills of Spiritual Intelligence*. Brilliantly outlining exactly what spiritual intelligence is, completely separate from any theological or religious affiliation, she writes of its application to leaders and corporate cultures. Amid the details of how we are all capable of growing and sustaining spiritual intelligence in the workplace in addition to IQ and EQ (emotional intelligence), she believes women don't have a fast line to higher development, nor do men have a slow line to it. "The patriarchy," she said in our interview, "has warped both."

The implication then is that both masculine and feminine qualities in leadership and organizations are virtuous, needed, and helpful. Without them, women well over fifty find ourselves rapidly disengaging now more than ever.

Across the board, we are all witnessing the worn limits of patriarchal systems.

Of course, organizations are created to produce things—either products or services—and good business leaders know there must be a strategy, systems, processes, a culture, good leadership, and clear communication to achieve a profit. Profits are necessary and honorable. As a systems expert, I support companies and not-for-profits showing proof of their utility; outcomes that manifest their mission. In so doing, companies must systematize behaviors and practices that respect the whole person and what he/she needs in order to do her best at work. Values, decision-making processes, communication channels, evaluations and promotions, physical layouts and structures, assignments, access to mentors, and many other criteria all factor in to how/if an environment is patriarchal (in its negative form) or conscious, balanced, and triple or quadruple bottom lined.

Again, patriarchal is not a gender categorization, it's a type of environment that becomes sustained over time by informal and formal practices.

"What's most important is to have the world work for 100 percent of humanity without ecological offense or the disadvantage of anyone," said Christine McDougall, fifty-eight, founder of 223AM.com and convener of multiple design projects under the name Big Blue Sky on the Gold Coast of Australia. "We cannot dismiss, malign, or throw out young men. It's complementarianism that will bring what's needed. How do we find the humanistic and soulful way of working together?"

Interviewee Susan Cannon, fifty-seven, was a successful corporate executive in a male-dominated industry who is introduced in more detail later. Together with her colleague Suzanne Anderson, Susan realized years ago that there were no leadership models for women, but rather the expectation that women would conform to the masculine model. Absent this important model, they set off to develop one! Ten years in the trenches, learning from experience, from coaching women, from developing university curriculum and programs, they wrote a book of the deep synthesis they had learned and integrated. *The Way of the Mysterial Woman* is a book they consider a gift at this historic time of challenge and transformation. I consider it one, also.

This issue is no small matter for the women I interviewed and, I suspect, millions of others who are over fifty and acutely aware of the state of our cultural systems in general. Voices were loud and declarative on this far-reaching pattern shift: we are Done With being part of imbalanced worlds of work, policy, pay, and programs. We may indeed shout! Not at the walls that wish to keep us limited and producing, but about the new models needed to replace the old.

GIVING AND GIVING...AND GIVING

Some permutations of imbalanced systems, including behavioral ones, happen in everyday culture, outside the walls of companies.

One is an often-taught slogan "It is better to give than to receive."

At first glance, I and many women I interviewed agree with this principle. When it's expressed as compassionate caring-in-action, giving to others in need is right and good. Taken as a carte blanche, however, women are sometimes taught that it is their primary role to give...and give...and give...and give. If self is not taken into account—also giving compassion, time, gentle affection, and care to ourselves—we are worn thin by a life of other orientation.

Interviewee thandiwe, sixty-six, doesn't mince words about it.

"It's better to give than receive is bullshit," she said. "Receiving is also a gift." As thandiwe talked about the inextricable link between giving and receiving, she added, "We have to be mindful of the programming that giving is superior and separate than receiving. When we appreciatively receive, we allow the giver the joy of their giving. TV and other media say women should put everyone else before themselves—but what is the difference between self-care and selfishness? It's not selfish to take care of ourselves!" Her voice of savvy experience was notable. "Self-care is right to do. We need compassion for ourselves just as we need it for others."

We are Done With cultural messaging suggesting we should starve our own needs to feed others' needs—including the organizations we work for.

We are also Done With our loved youngers taking that message on—especially younger women. We want a different reality for them. We want to mentor them and communicate to them that in the long run, always giving does NOT achieve what is good for ourselves, our families, our relationships, nor our work.

"You run into enough brick walls—you've done enough—that finally you need to attend to what's important in your life. You realize you can say 'no,'" said Karen, sixty-one, from her home in Australia. "You have knowledge, experience, and a mature perspective that gives you freedom."

At this stage of life, there has to be balance. In fact, it's nonnegotiable. And if we're not heard on this front, women over fifty walk away to find new arenas in which to contribute.

It should be noted that this is a very different premise than someone who may say, "You owe me something" or "If I don't get my way, I'll walk out the door." The distinction is important. This Done With That premise in *A Call to Further Becoming* is based on twenty, thirty, forty years of having been in the work trenches—at the "bleeding edge," as Rosemary, age seventy-seven, called it.

Unfortunately, bleeding-edge stories are quite common to women.

Joyce, fifty-seven, joined her Florida-based company as a mid-level manager in the IT department. Joyce was self-directed and smart. She brought new ideas and a passion for process improvement, both of which led to several promotions. When the company purchased several other businesses and more than doubled in size, Joyce was put in charge of aligning its disjointed systems and upgrading their IT capacity across the board at the same time.

In other words, the entire company and its effective running were on her shoulders.

Completing the work under budget and before the deadline, Joyce was surprised to learn the male colleagues at her level had received raises while she did not. The only woman now at a VP level, she spoke with the CEO who, she said, "waved her off" and suggested her worth was not assessed in the same way since she provided internal support.

Joyce had already taken note of the dinners, trips, and golf outings she was not included in with her male colleagues and the CEO. "I loved my work and was being recognized for it in my industry, even if not internally by my boss."

She was also widely respected in her company by her own IT employees and by the departments who benefitted from her innovative changes.

But over the years, as she sat in numerous senior leader meetings, she noticed how her opinions were rarely acknowledged. "I grew tired of being treated like I was invisible," she said. "I knew that company inside and out—but was expected to act as a subordinate to many of the inflated egos on that team. I was expected to just be nice."

Not surprisingly, Joyce submitted her resignation. She established her own company doing exactly the same work on a contract basis for many companies who welcomed her experience and leading-edge capabilities.

"I am so done with feeding that male 'We are in charge' ego nonsense," she summarized in our interview. "I feel 100 percent in my integrity though it has not been easy. I'm surrounded by people I trust, and I give them what I didn't get from my CEO. I'll take this road any day."

In the age of active wisdom, we are clearly Done With environments that are not pro-humanity, including ourselves.

Marie Wilson, age seventy-seven, was involved at the highest levels of the feminist movement in its early days. As an author, political organizer and entrepreneur, Marie founded the White House Project and the Ms. Foundation for Women. She has trained and empowered over 15,000 diverse women to run for office. Remember "Take Your Daughter to Work Day"? My daughter Lilly and I owe those wonderful experiences to Marie's brainchild in 1992.

After a lifetime of powerhouse work on behalf of women and still advocating politically in her late seventies, Marie's extraordinary perspective, shared in our interview, is that three blended elements—work, family, and leisure—must be present at every stage of life, especially for women, if we're to lead healthy, happy lives. Marie believes these elements will most likely be found in systems that also seek diverse voices; systems that make concerted efforts to respect experienced perspectives, especially perspectives that challenge historically unchallenged centers of power. In other words, the voices of women. And organizations that create products or services that benefit, and do not harm, people and the natural world.

We see in our daughters and those whom we mentor that the pace, expectations, and cultural messaging is unhealthy and even frantic for younger women. This may finally be changing…slowly…but it's been a very long time coming.

But being Done With it ourselves (because we know better), we are prone to pass along new and different messages, new and different systems that support and benefit women in their roles as leaders, mothers, partners, and life livers.

After decades of advocating for laws, structures, and norms that facilitate good and progress for everyone—and pushing against policies and practices that disinvite or kill these higher values, experience has led huge numbers of women well over fifty to say: *Here's where I'm willing to place my energy—and here's where I'm Done With placing my energy.*

Story

Cecile Ortiz, sixty-six, has always been an advocate for people. Her mother was her model. Part of a family who emigrated from Mexico and with only a fifth-grade education, Cec's Mom had seven children and lived the theme that "community was not for someone else to create." When immigrant families crossed over the river from Mexico, brought by coyotes with agreement of the white farmers who wanted their labor, the neighbors would say to Cec's mother, "Rosie, would you take this family in?"

It was second nature for Cec to leave her own bed and make room for the new arrivees. Her mother, she said, was "always a community worker."

When Cec went to college in Boulder, total culture shock set in. The institution wanted Latina students, and she wanted to attend. But coming from a tight community where family was everything, she couldn't get a grasp on this independently oriented environment. "I totally failed at University of Colorado," she said. Not from lack of intellectual capability but from cultural alienation. After marrying and giving birth to her two sons, Cec navigated what she called her "learning years." She found a mentor—her Latino boss—and has never forgotten how important it is to have someone who believes in you.

Cec's professional path led her to become director at Mi Casa, a not-for-profit providing services to help the underrepresented constituents in the Latino community become trained and self-reliant. A staunch advocate for Latina women especially, Cec's compelling efforts provide counseling and create avenues for education and progress to the clients she served caught the attention of none other than the Ms. Foundation. Remember Marie Wilson who founded the Ms. Foundation? Cec's organization was not only awarded monetary grants and special training from the Ms. Foundation to expand Mi Casa's efforts further, but Cec herself received the Ms. Foundation Award!

I absolutely loved coming across the intersection of their stories in my interviews! Cec was a prime example of how one woman's passion-in-action created powerful progress for others.

With wind beneath her wings and back to school to successfully earn a business and international studies degree, Cec was poised to move into larger arenas with the hard-earned, practical, and savvy experience she had.

Moving into government to work on policies from the governor's office, including oversight of the Women's Business Office and later in various director and deputy director positions, Cec described her aim as "trying to be a reformer within the system."

Readers will no doubt recognize the thunder in those words: A woman of color. A history of high-touch community work. A trailblazer on the front lines. And now in a government system in order to *reform*.

Not surprisingly, here is where Cec learned her most valuable lessons.

First: "It truly is a patriarchy," she stated flatly about governmental bureaucracy.

Second, she added, "We as women have a different kind of power: the power of observation. Since we've been outside the primary power circle for a long time, it's given us the opportunity to observe. That's relevant. As a result, we can lead really well."

Leading for Cec at high levels in state government meant a growing awareness of what she was Done With. She developed the willingness to speak from that place. At first intimidated by titles and PhD-level colleagues, Cec observed, sometimes held back, but slowly recognized the value of her wisdom, foresight, decision making, and ability to see broad-scale patterns of policy implications. Sitting in air-conditioned meeting rooms, she could picture exactly how their conversations and votes would benefit or fail the Coloradans they were serving.

In other words, Cec had earned the unique perspective of a Pioneer.

"I became Done With second-guessing myself," she shared in our interview. "I finally believed in my own wisdom. I grew beyond sitting in silence even though there were risks of being seen as a 'loose cannon' or someone who couldn't be controlled; who didn't follow norms."

"As women," she continued, "we have to walk across that bridge of speaking up."

Cec's resilience and compassionate integrity culminated in what can only be called new and pioneering leadership: a blend of feminine and masculine qualities that defy established patriarchal ways and get things done with the betterment of humanity in mind. She mentioned the great need for honesty in rooms of power, and her aim to speak up from a place of love.

And what does that sound like in Done With That terms from Cec?

"If they haven't done their own work and I'm asked to go in and save them, I say no."

"If I'm in a room and I can't make a difference, I don't stay."

"If being there is only because that's what success looks like, I don't go."

These days, Cec said she picks her battles carefully.

She chooses the three rather than ten things she'll focus on. She makes sure others are doing their work too. "I also have my 'kitchen cabinet'—my support network," she added. "We really need this when we're working in patriarchal systems."

The bottom line about what she has learned in the Done With That domain?

1. Speak up from the place of feminine observation and knowing. Others will reach out privately and say they're glad you did.
2. If it's not the right battle, don't take it on. If they aren't willing to hear your input, consider changing environments. She said, "Being in places and fighting in places where I don't fit—I don't need to do that anymore."
3. Don't ever compromise who you are.
4. "I am absolutely who I am now from learning this," she concluded happily. "My main work is that I have to be Cec."

QUOTES

"I'm worn out with hierarchical relationships, competitive approaches, and political environments. It doesn't work to be told at this stage that I can't have input in my annual goals! I'm done with having to

be careful of what I say because of big egos and being surrounded by a masculine, male-dominated approach to everything. I know too much now."

—MARTHA N., FIFTY-SIX

"The number of people who have been asked to come back to work after a baby is born, or after receiving a shattering diagnosis, or experiencing a death—these are times when life goes on at a different pace and should. The formal systems won't be of support when a crisis hits. Young women really need to know this. We need to provide it for ourselves and also demand that employers care about us as much as they do their profits. Women are needed to call this out."

—MAGGIE W., SIXTY-TWO

"There are political machinations in academia—an example of which was one of the governing bodies I was on and chaired for six years. The stress of the politics began to manifest itself in my body. I took a sabbatical and realized I don't have to fix everything. I can walk away. It's important to know your strengths and know your value. Know what you want to do and what you don't. I am doing exactly what I want to do at that institution after all the years of contributing because I took a stand. That's what strength looks like now."

—ANNETTE T., SIXTY-TWO

Antidote To

This Declaration is an antidote to often unchallenged cultural expectations, especially for women, about how worth is to be measured. It thwarts the narrative of centuries that subtly suggests we should "muscle on" in outdated systems or live out scripts that do not serve our own and others' good. The feminine way is not ego-based entitlement but deep honoring of where our personal energy is worthy to be applied for the sake of further good for ourselves and in the world around us, and to move in that direction, no matter what is left behind.

PRACTICE

There are places (like offices), events (like conferences), activities (like auditing, commuting, keyboarding, standing, or sitting for hours), relational constellations (like reporting to someone, supervising others, being on a team) and "props" (like computers, sewing machines, dance shoes, flip chart markers) that your whole being may say you are Done With. You may not have distaste, dislike, or disdain toward these things, exactly. As one woman in this chapter asked, "Is it possible to still like my job but want to leave it?" Or another who said, "I loved it right up to the day I retired, but knew for a year it was time to go—and I never grieved; never looked back." It's sometimes the awareness that we're just done, like An who arranged a gathering to give away her multicolored markers after realizing she didn't want to conduct any more training workshops.

The inner calling about what we're ready to close is as important as what we're ready to open.

- What do you know you're Done With?
- What are the signs, subtle as they may be?
- Are you Done With tangible things (like a particular job) or intangible things (like doing other people's work for them or saying yes to every committee request you get)?
- Does your Done With have a strong declaration to it? With whom can you share it—either loudly, or quietly like an important secret?
- What ritual could you do to mark the dismissal of what you're Done With?
- What step can you take today to either declare it, ritualize it, or both?

Standing in what you are Done With is liberating. Don't underestimate it. It can take tremendous courage and surrender. I cheer you on to listen and honor this inner knowing when it arrives.

DECLARATION 4

ANVIL OF OUR BECOMING

We are learning to value lessons learned from our trials and challenges.

When we reach a certain point in our lives, we are bound to ask ourselves who we are, whether we have done enough, and yes—whether we are worthy. No matter how illogical and unfair this self-questioning may seem, some of us well recognize its presence, even if it knocks at our door only once or twice.

From my interviews, I have come to believe that the questioning of our worthiness is far more present and pervasive than we might guess.

On my wall are three words I vowed this book would do: affirm, inform, inspire.

And notice which one comes first.

These words represent what the 100 women I interviewed wished for their sisters at this stage. The fervor of their input was especially strong about wanting me to convey the value of each woman's life—the irreplaceable uniqueness each woman possesses—and that her one-of-a-kind journey is worthy simply by being its own unique story of becoming.

How important that we recognize our worth related to *being* and *becoming* as opposed to simply what we've *done*.

Martie, seventy-three, voiced a profound truth echoed by ninety-nine others and familiar in my bones, too. "It's not our achievements that form us," she said. "Our responses to trials and challenges do. They are the Anvil of our Becoming." Shock, loss, injustice, heartbreak, indignity, betrayal, competition, deception, illness, fatigue, marginalization, and myriad more minutiae of the human condition have demanded living the definition of resilience and, hopefully, grace. Events that have stopped us in our tracks have helped wake us up, plant our trust in something larger, recognize natural (and unnatural) rhythms of life that sooner or later require our alignment, and tap capacities we never knew we had.

This is worthy work.

The drama is not the point. It's what it takes to emerge.

As I write this, I ask myself why the Anvil of Our Becoming deserves its own legs upon which to stand as one of the ten Declarations. Scanning the collective body of 100 stories and the voices that told them, I'm humbled by the magnitude of meaning behind lives sewn back together, patient stitch-by-stitch or step-by-step, when loss or vulnerability have threatened to shatter any belief in the existence of goodness, truth, and beauty.

Standing on the other side, having invested in reflecting and claiming the humble lessons we've learned, we find ourselves at new altitudes of perspective. With new eyes we may say: *This is who I am now; this is how I see.* These new altitudes position us to lead—and lead in a way that balances what needs to get done with the natural laws of balance that allow us to thrive as well as produce.

The process of becoming who we are is often not the result of roads we expected or roadblocks we wanted. Of course, part of our becoming has indeed been by happy decisions we've made and choices that proved progressive and joyous. But it's usually a mix. What the women I interviewed reported in the majority of cases was that the biggest breakthroughs for reaching a better self were from the most intense challenges and biggest relinquishments. There appears to be a shedding we go through, sometimes many times related to many layers of superficial identity, to find the new us-ness on the other side.

To me, this process is a feminine one. Letting go. Tremendous humility in facing what is facing us. Relinquishment of whatever we may have assumed was reliable, or to which we were attached. Some sort of reckoning. And a resulting shift. Otto Scharmer in U-Theory calls this the "letting go/letting come."[6]

Betty Artes, sixty-two in New Mexico knows about letting go and letting come. She began her story with saying, "We immigrated from Argentina. What courage my mother had! It gave me a foundation for the roller coaster of life. I finished college early—married, had a son. My company fast-tracked me. I made pioneering moves—bought a house. I was going 100 miles an

---

6   Otto Scharmer, *The Essentials of U-Theory: Core Principles and Applications* (Oakland, CA: Berrett Koehler Publishers, 2018).

hour. Then I had a car accident. A head injury. It was absolutely a wake-up call," Betty said. She realized that the pursuit of Spirit was the most important thing. Prior to this, Betty said, she hadn't believed in a Higher Force. But the wake-up call made her more spiritual.

"All of it said: STOP. After that, my life became so much more intentional; so much more rewarding."

Shortly after, Betty was asked to join a restaurant business. "I said, 'It's going to be about creating a family atmosphere for the staff.' The guests could see it and feel it. We made everyone feel welcome."

"The business didn't give me happiness," Betty continued. "It was just a vehicle to do good. It was all about the people." Betty lamented the way society equates value with "net worth." She said she's learned to "set that aside and say, 'Just shine that light.' The rest will come."

HONORING OUR ANVILS

Wisdom is borne of bending low and finding ourselves servants to what will save us. From here our becoming continues, however meager the victories.

Small victories can be mighty. The deep knowing I heard in my 100 interviews was spoken quietly, without fanfare. It was anything but self-aggrandized. It was reflective of feminine qualities so needed in leadership today: compassionate, humble, rock-solid gravitas without privilege or pontification. In fact, many women, when they heard their own voices speak spontaneously about lessons derived from their own stories, were touched to the core by what they heard themselves say.

"If I have a realization after speaking all this, it's knowing what a miracle we all are," said design strategist Maggie Weiss, age sixty-two.

"That every woman could know the preciousness and importance of her life," said sixty-three-year-old Fiona Vincent, who heads an award-winning UK consultancy and is also the coordinator of a nonprofit, anti-plastics factory campaign in her region of Ireland. "We should not underestimate the difference every one of us makes."

Sunny, sixty-three, who we meet later, added, "To speak about my life has been so empowering. So validating. There's some bittersweet-ness to it, recognizing the losses. But there's a kick-ass knowing: here I am. I'm still here! And—I'm still in the arena, doing it."

After speaking about her personal Anvil of Becoming, one interviewee confided, "I'm weepy and I don't know why."

Why are we so moved by the lessons we've learned from our trials and challenges?

- First, because something deep within us is reminded of what life is really all about: loving, learning, continuing to become, and the legacy of the way we have done so.
- Second, because no one told us that!
- Third, because the process of this becoming is buried in importance alongside the process of doing.
- Fourth, because the patriarchal architecture around us has separated the inseparable—being and doing, becoming and expressing—and built systems around just one piece.
- Fifth, as a result of the above, we haven't the cultural spaces

to identify, reflect upon, and metabolize our challenges and the subsequent wisdom and successes. (See chapter 5, "Self-Witnessing in Solitude" and chapter 7, "Create a Moai" for more on how to do this.) Exacerbating this in my view is a decrease in church attendance where metabolizing can and should take place. I believe this decrease is partly, but not wholly, for reasons of patriarchal theologies and systems that don't stand up to rigorous thinking and feminine intuition. I am grateful beyond measure that my own church, founded by a woman, has always withstood the test of both. But I may be in the minority.

- And sixth, because women have not been encouraged and provided avenues to honor the preciousness of their lives and the "enough-ness" of who we are right here, right now.

Christina Baldwin, seventy, is author of seven books including two classic contributions to "the renaissance of personal writing" and is founder of a journaling movement beginning in 1990. She has also been a seminar presenter for over thirty years and a leading voice in the arena of group dialogue and reflection that speaks of the importance of knowing where we've been and, from it, who we are. When I asked her opinion on the highest good that could come from a book like this one, she responded, "That those who may not see themselves as pioneers can claim their empowerment and claim their voices."

So many women over fifty have done so much, without taking time to claim the natural laws of progress we've successfully earned.

"I wasn't raised to be a leader," said Betsy Marlow, sixty-eight. "I was more passive, so I didn't see myself that way. Then my husband died and I had to be a grown-up!—I had to learn how to run a nonprofit in order to sustain myself. I just retired as CEO after twelve years. Now I know: you can do anything you have to do or want to do."

Perhaps we don't see ourselves as leaders, newsmakers, business-people, pioneers until someone points out what we've overcome or immigrated from → to. There are many names the 100 women I interviewed used to describe how they see themselves and others at this stage. Some of them may resonate for readers.

Yelder is one. "A young elder in training," Gigi Coyle, sixty-six, occasionally calls herself in addition to guide or mentor, depending on who she's with. Gigi, whom I profile in more detail later, not only offers the word yelder as a role with younger women, but also as a way to view ourselves as we pioneer new identities at this stage.

Maga is another. "The maga stage means 'wise women,'" said Heather, eighty-one, an author and Rolfer®, whom we will meet a bit later, "active in the world after menopause and after children have left."

Sage. Space Holder. Crone. Priestess. OWL (older wise learner).

Marni Harmony, Unitarian Universalist (UU) minister, dubs us as living in "the Fifth Season." She defines "Fifth Season" as "a time in life when one is experienced and seasoned, not moving into decline but rather a wholly new and open season yet to be defined."

Naming aside, it's the *nature* of who we are that's deserving. How we've derived our identity to this point. The Anvil of Our Becoming is worth honoring and claiming. And no one but us is going to do it.

Nancy, sixty-four, has done such claiming from the bottom up.

"I was in a wretched place," she said. "Alcoholic, married to an alcoholic. I decided to ramp up a spiritual practice and therapy, and I flirted with AA. I left my twenty-year marriage and the property I had gardened and created as a paradise. That was a loss, but I knew I must leave. I had an inner desire to downsize, downsize, downsize. I moved into an efficiency and threw myself into Twelve Steps. Recovery was my whole focus for a while, while I worked as a librarian in a mid-security prison. The miracle was finding God in community. AA was my sangha (a Sanskrit word meaning 'community'). I've been sober four years now.

Nancy now does meditation, yoga, and daily workouts. "My life is about any service I can give," she said. "It's been an honor to see so many women in the prison system where I work who have overcome things. I'm about to retire and travel in my Ford Transit. I will have a community along the way: SERVAS (people with whom I will stay for mutual fellowship) and AA. It may seem self-indulgent, but I want it to have a service element to it, making contact with women along the way who I can be in service to."

Detour

I took a long time getting here,
much of it wasted on wrong turns,
back roads riddled by ruts.
I had adventures
I never would have known
if I proceeded as the crow flies.
Super highways are so sure
of where they are going:
they arrive too soon.
A straight line isn't always
the shortest distance

between two people.
Sometimes I act as though
I'm heading somewhere else
while, imperceptibly,
I narrow the gap between you and me.
I'm not sure I'll ever
know the right way, but I don't mind
getting lost now and then.
Maps don't know everything.

—RUTH FELDMAN[7]

WHEN DEVASTATIONS ARE OUR ANVILS

Sometimes a woman's warrior-like fiber is further fortified by facing obstacles. Sometimes one moment of courageous decisioning has been a profound determinant of what will follow for many years.

Other times the suffocating blanket of bad tidings has been transcended by a woman's indomitable quest for a breakthrough to joy. None of us have done it alone; though alone is what it may look like from the outside. Every hard corner turned has been attended by reaching deeply within, out, or up.

A favorite hymn I grew up with said "Loss is gain."[8] Admittedly, I didn't understand that in my younger years and mentally filed it in a folder called Rainbows and Butterflies—or what Robert Augus-

7 Ruth Feldman, "Detour," in *The Ambition of Ghosts* (University Center, MI: Green River Press, 1979).

8 Mary Baker Eddy, "Mother's Evening Prayer," *Christian Science Hymnal* (Boston, MA: The Christian Science Publishing Society, 1932, renewed 1960).

tus Masters calls "spiritual bypassing."[9] I now see its profound truth. It isn't the losses themselves. Those can feel devastating. It is the emergence from them, sometimes from desperation, sometimes from pure faith that there must be something to learn, sometimes from the seeming miracles that arrive in their midst, reminding us that good is still present.

One interviewee, who asked not to be named, spoke about the challenge she faced as a single mother, working full time, when her daughter was diagnosed with a mental illness. She recalled standing in a courtroom a few years back with her daughter in chains, having "an unshakable conviction that Love would rule the nightmarish moment of her inhumane imprisonment in a chillingly uncaring system." Enacting the courage to speak up in court for her daughter's release, holding a conviction that God/Higher Power would rule this situation, she witnessed a shift in the courtroom scene. People came to her daughter's aid. She was tended to by a nurse and released to a compassionate outcome.

"Nothing can shake my world now," said this interviewee. "No professional accolade comes close to what that did to my being."

While some of the trials we've faced have been up close and personal, others have been in association with our loved ones who have faced extreme circumstances. Or we've been in racial/ethnic groups where historical and prejudicial injustice are an unavoidable part of life.

"I find myself by recognizing the whole of what I've experienced and why," said one woman of color, "and the coming home I feel

---

9   Robert Augustus Masters, *Spiritual Bypassing: When Spirituality Disconnects Us from What Really Matters* (Berkeley: North Atlantic Books, 2010).

when using that knowledge to educate and bolster others who are going through the same experience."

"My son passed two years ago," said Ann Linnea, sixty-seven, who we meet in more detail later. "You don't take anything for granted. Things have become clearer and sharper since Brian died. I've always been involved with projects that are Earth based, spending a lot of time outdoors and writing about it. Now there's more spaciousness with it. It connects me to something larger than myself. Everything is deeper since he passed. I stand in wonder and awe of creation around me."

If indeed "loss is gain"—if our trials and devastations are the Anvils of Our Becoming—then this alone is a message we have to give to our loved youngers along with the tremendous worth of our lives resiliently lived.

Of course, while we reach the "Fifth Season" (as Marni spoke of earlier) due to years on this earth, that does not alone make wisdom a given! There must also be the capacity to reflect upon and transmit our lessons and to continue learning.

The women I interviewed had this capacity in spades. In their commitment to continued becoming, they recognized the value of harvesting the lessons from life events so far and using past and present challenges as fodder for transformation. They were all drawn toward higher altitudes of perspective as a result.

We deserve to honor the Anvil of Our Becoming for ourselves. For each other. For the generations that follow us. For the world.

Story

June Munger, Japanese American, offered many outbursts of infectious laughter during our hour together. Coming up on seventy years old, she described herself as a "stay-at-home mom" most of her adult life. She is also a cancer survivor, a recovered closed-head injury patient, the wife of a spouse with cancer who also has Parkinson's, and...a ukulele player. Of those many things, there was *one* she most wanted to talk about.

"With all the life threats going on around me, I had to find an escape. I saw an ad for a ukulele group at my Pilates studio. I started with that, then took lessons and absolutely loved it. I realize having fun is a spiritual practice. Being happy is what makes life good. Playing the ukulele has been a life saver to me! You know, you can't play the blues on a ukulele!"

"When I was in chemo I gave myself ten minutes to wallow; to get it out of my system. Then I got on with it. We have to acknowledge the dark side of things, but we keep going for the light."

June recalled attending a recent ukulele conference "where everyone was moving and happy and full of life." But then she came home to a depressed husband battling his illness. June had an inspiration then. I said, "'Let's move to Port Townsend (Washington) where they have the big ukulele community.' We both said yes. We sold our house, met a realtor there, and found a house in less than five hours."

"We never need to shut ourselves in a box no matter how difficult things get. We know how to be brave and embrace the choices we have. We can do the best we can with what we have."

When June's husband passed away one year ago, June attended a ukulele festival three weeks later, dedicating a song to him which she played during open mic time. Several people were moved to tears. "The healing I felt," June said, "was also felt by those around me. I am playing and singing as part of my new life."

June had a few other words of inspiration for women over fifty: "Loss is part of life, but not the main focus of life. Appreciate yourself every minute. And share what you know with others—as they say in Hawaii, 'Talk story.'"

Then she let out a laugh. "And get a ukulele. You just can't be depressed."

QUOTES

"In my life, tragedy has turned into gifts. Whatever blocks or trouble or pain, I face it. Not intellectually; I've had to take the essential feelings and stand in them fully. I studied various techniques and rites of passage and traditions. I've become a teacher of them. I've stepped beyond family and cultural conditioning. It all comes from a deeper place now. It's been a spiritual path—a surrendering. As a result, I'm in a place where whatever I do fulfills every part of me because of the life lessons—a gift from within the wound."

—PIPPA B., SIXTY-FIVE

"I married an alcoholic. When I left him it was one of the most difficult steps of my life. In Al Anon, I sang the blues, and they said, "It's you, not all of them." That was a major marker. It changed my life. I had to examine myself. I went back to school, eventually got a PhD. I found contemplative spiritual teaching along the way and started meditating. Later, I experienced another relationship breakup; someone I thought would become my husband was living a deceptive life. I left the city where we lived, left my work, moved, and delved deeply

into more personal growth. Doorways opened. I learned that PTSD can actually be Post Traumatic Growth Syndrome. It's a polarity, but extreme difficulties are extreme openings for new meaning and new ways of being. Success is not what the culture tells us it is. To put some grace in the world, to hold space for others, is what gives me meaning and purpose."

—NAME WITHHELD

Antidote To

This Declaration is an antidote to undervaluing the worth of our individual lives and the magnitude of our "becoming," however hard it has been. We are enough, just as we are.

PRACTICE

For this exercise, you'll need at least twenty minutes. Write or audio record from the following prompts:

1. Identify a challenge you've had in your life; one that did not look positive or promising on its face. It might be something that was unexpected, something that turned out to be bigger than you expected. Focus on one that occurred after age fifty. What was it? How did it come about?
2. How did you feel initially at the time of change?
3. What was the eventual outcome?
4. What steps did you take during the challenge? What thoughts or beliefs prompted those particular steps? How were they helpful?
5. What did you learn about yourself?
6. How has the learning influenced your life?
7. What would you say to other women who may be facing a similar change in their lives right now?

Answers to these reflective questions, especially number five, hint at how powerfully we are formed—and transformed—by the innate inner resources we discover and deep lessons we've developed from our trials. Our surrounding culture exalts "winning the Oscar" and all that it implies—but victories won behind the curtain and during the rehearsals are the ones that form us into who we are.

SELF-WITNESSING IN SOLITUDE

We are learning to listen to the quiet within and to God/Spirit.

Like many women, I've kept a journal for the last twenty years. While cleaning out my closet months ago, I came across a loose-leaf page with faded writing; a journal entry from my mid-fifties. The title across the top said, "What I know for sure."

> *I absolutely love the quiet of the morning. It is sustaining and delicious. It feeds my bones. And it feeds my soul. To have the quiet disturbed with the onslaught of talk or the demand of activity would be anathema to my rhythm. Living my truth means withdrawal from many other things, like noisy socializing and travel during heavy traffic, but I cannot do otherwise.*

At that time, I honestly thought I was in a minority of people who find the potent quiet of early morning essential to life. The first ninety minutes of the morning, alone with my thoughts and two sacred practices, including prayer, has been the most grounding part of my day for at least twenty-five years. It has everything to do with the way my day flows. When I take time for disciplined listening and study, the way I'm to Pioneer On is clearer and more harmonious.

What I learned in the 100 interviews with women over fifty is that I'm not alone in this at all. In fact, nearly all the women I spoke with find time for solitude almost as important as food and air at this point in their lives.

How did I come across this fascinating and, for me, unexpected theme? I found it out when asking one of my favorite interview questions: *What nonnegotiable practices, rituals, or structures do you have that help you do and be what you're doing and being right now?*

I anticipated hearing about good sleeping and eating habits, exercise, reading, and perhaps some religious practices. But after the first dozen interviews, I realized that each woman had mentioned the word *solitude* or *quiet time* combined with details about how she uses that time. Then twenty more interviews revealed the same thing. I reached what Brené Brown calls in her research "high saturation" where it's statistically significant that a theme has emerged.

CRITICAL AND LIFE GIVING—NOT JUST A "NICE-TO-HAVE"

I remember interviewing Katie Eastman, fifty-five, who was one of the most extraverted women I had the joy of speaking with. With a PsyD under her belt, Katie is an active and involved mother and wife, while also running a therapy practice and working on a major media project. I asked her this same question: "What nonnegotiable practices do you have that help you do and be all that you're doing and being right now, Katie?"

In her enthusiastic, full-of-spunk voice she responded without a moment's hesitation. "Oh, I can tell you. Quiet, quiet, quiet, and QUIET!"

To be clear, when the women I interviewed spoke about their desire for solitude, they weren't talking about doing transactional activities alone such as running errands, shopping, work tasks. They spoke of this quiet as a dimension of spiritual practice; a receptive state of mind that listens beyond the ear. It involves arranging to be in a physical setting where mental chatter can be cleared. This allows thoughts to arrive from what I call "Divine Mind, Love"—some would say from God, Source. Women used different words, but each word conveyed a spiritual presence beyond ourselves. For some women, the messages or guidance they get involves what they should or should not do. At times it's about hearing how to take the next step. For many, the silence helps us continue evolving, becoming.

I loved hearing how the late novelist, playwright, psychotherapist, and poet Paul Goodman wrote about nine types of silence in his book *Speaking and Language*.[10]

"There is the dumb silence of slumber or apathy; the sober silence that goes with a solemn animal face; the fertile silence of awareness, pasturing the soul, whence emerge new thoughts; the alive silence of alert perception, ready to say, "This...this..."; the musical silence that accompanies absorbed activity; the silence of listening to another speak, catching the drift and helping him

---

10   Paul Goodman, *Speaking and Language* (Surrey, UK: Wildwood House Lmtd, 1973).

be clear; the noisy silence of resentment and self-recrimination, loud and subvocal speech but sullen to say it; baffled silence; the silence of peaceful accord with other persons or communion with the cosmos."

The women I interviewed were speaking of the "fertile silence of awareness," "alive silence of alert perception," and "peaceful accord…with the cosmos." Inhabiting this type of silence—these magnificent moments with Soul's stillness—necessitates arranging and maintaining such times purposefully.

Ann Masai Jones, sixty-nine, who goes by masai (lowercase purposeful) is still actively teaching racial/social justice/leadership at the college level. She said this: "I spend quiet time with myself several hours a day. If I don't have it, I'm discombobulated. I practice meditation, contemplation, drawing, and writing. I feel it's my number one job to show up as my authentic self in all areas of life…and solitude each day is essential to being able to do so."

Like masai, many women spoke about their commitment to receptive solitude in association with other practices. Corollary practices—like writing and drawing for masai—invite and further enhance the spiritual downloads these 100 women talked about.

Hearing the "cocktail of practices"—the unique bundle of things we do in the sanctuary of this private time with self and Spirit—was one of the most delightful parts of the whole interview process for me. How creative we are! How attuned we are to what brings us into the peaceful sanctuary of silence's sacredness. And how consecrated we are to stay with what allows us to enter this space.

In order of frequency mentioned, the top four practices women engage during times of planned quiet are:

1. Meditation or prayer.
2. Walking in nature.
3. Journaling.
4. Reading, including sacred texts, essays, inspirational quotes, and poetry.

Overall, there is something remarkable about the simplicity and orderliness by which we as women over fifty engage the practice of listening to self and to Source. The relief of quiet is perhaps partly a balancing dynamic to decades of taking care of others and juggling a myriad of roles, often without having taken time for ourselves in the mix. It's not just a nice luxury to have at this point in life. For many of us, it is absolutely essential.

Self-Witnessing in Solitude takes on a different look from one woman to another. But each one involves engaging an inner sense of quiet. Its purpose is consistent across the board as an avenue to:

- Hear ourselves.
- Honor our inner voice.
- Get aligned with Love, God (or whatever name one uses for Higher Power).
- Feel grounded and centered.
- Satisfy the soul.
- Reaffirm connection with the oneness of Spirit and diminish separation.
- Drop into the presence of peace.

SELF-WITNESSING AS PRAYER

"I do daily meditation and daily writing," said author Pam Noble, seventy-four, a nature poet and essayist, vision quest guide, retired psychotherapist, and workshop facilitator. "Getting out in nature is also nonnegotiable. Being in the natural world is a medicine walk for me."

Pam continued, "It's all done from a posture of listening. As women, we must listen first to ourselves. We have everything we need to be who we were created to be. We must listen for our own wisdom; look within for it. A practice I have is the sense of being seen by Other—that is, who is seeing me? and then claiming the wisdom of what the Divine Other is seeing."

Pam's practice of seeing herself as the Divine Other sees her is, in my view, an active form of prayer. My own daily practice since the time I was in college has been to read a Bible-based lesson with corollary passages from *Science and Health*[11] reminding me that we are created spiritually and are innately good. It provides a pure lens through which I try to see things every day.

At fifty-five, consulting company founder and entrepreneur Marie Peters's solo time is from a special chair she has in her home, situated to enjoy soft beautiful lighting she has set up that surrounds her where she sits. "Everywhere I look is beautiful," she said. "I do Centering Prayer and Lectio Divina readings [two Christian prayer practices] every day. I also journal. I can honestly say these things inform every part of my life."

Another interviewee, age seventy-one, said, "For me, it starts with a prayer. Then I have an ancestor practice. I practice time alone every day. I need the space."

---

11   Mary Baker Eddy, *Science and Health with Key to the Scriptures* (Boston, MA: Christian Science Publishing Society, 1875, renewed 1934), 506.

NATURE AS A GATEWAY

Many women find nature to deliver a soul feast unlike anything else. It's both a destination in which to experience solitude and a source of spiritual nourishment that elicits heightened listening and the kind of meditation that allows each moment to be complete in its present perfection. In nature, it seems, we find ourselves.

Listening to women speak about their nonnegotiable time in nature and reflecting on my own experience as a solo kayaker, it seems we feel ourselves sinking tap roots into something native to ourselves and our being.

"I start at 7 a.m. every day with a one-and-a-half-hour walk. I worship in the church of the blue sky!" said Vicki in her late sixties. Drawing upon her Native American background, she continued, "It's the center of my practice. I choose to be fully here, in the moment. It's a 'be with' practice. Everything is alive: the moose, mountain lions, bobcats, plants, animals. We humans have a unique gift; we can choose whether or not to be here in this moment. I remind myself during this time, 'Remember to be.'"

Gigi Coyle, age sixty-six, who has dedicated her whole life to community—to activism through the leading of specific processes which she names "circle ways, pilgrimage, and rites of passage"—said Solitude and Self-Witnessing are part of every curriculum in the programs and social profit organizations she has established. Co-creator of the Ojai Foundation and the School of Lost Borders, as well as three learning organizations and several far-reaching networks, she identifies nature as the primary teacher. "Wild nature speaks to us—it's a mirror for us to understand our own part in the big story," she said. "There is unending information, healing, and guidance available through our connection to the natural world."

GRATITUDE AS PRAYER AND PRACTICE

Gratitude was mentioned frequently as part of prayer, meditation, and also journaling. Many of us start our day with acknowledging good things and giving them the honor of being noticed and named. My two cousins and I, all into our sixties and spread across three US states, send daily text messages to each other about what we're grateful for that morning.

"I have a 'three good things' practice every morning. I review them from gratitude," said Susan Cannon, fifty-seven, author, futurist, adjunct professor, executive coach, and organizational innovation consultant. "Then I get outside. I run a mile, smelling, looking. I eat a good breakfast, meditate, and using my body as a tuning instrument I identify any tensions I have and clear them."

"I start by making my bed," said another interviewee at sixty-one. "Then I set my intentions for the day, meditate for one hour, and practice gratitude."

Dawna Markova, seventy-five, former senior affiliate of the Organizational Learning Center at MIT and now CEO of Professional Thinking Partners, is an internationally known expert in the fields of learning, perception, and asset focus. "The crazier it gets on the outside, the more important it is to go inside," said Dawna, who is also the beloved author of seventeen books. "For forty-five minutes every day I begin with gratitude," she said. "I sit by the river of my thoughts and choose which side of the story I'm going to follow: the rut story or the flowing river story."

SELF-WITNESSING AS A REGULAR PRACTICE

Overall, engaging inner quiet is a feminine impulse. Whether we do so walking through the woods, hiking alongside a creek or from a special chair at home, what emerges is a gift we give ourselves. The women I interviewed conveyed a conviction that their power starts from this place of connection to our best selves and to Something Larger. Available to men as much as to women, its practice gets short shrift on the list of things culturally lauded as achievements. Fortunately, there is a growing movement by individuals—and some companies—that attention to the domain loosely called "mindfulness" has direct bearing on bringing our best selves onto life's stage.

As a side note, there were several women with whom I spoke who referred to themselves as "inherently undisciplined" as Karen at sixty-one phrased it; not engaging in a regular practice of quiet or corollary activities of meditation or something similar. Some women said they have informal ways of listening throughout the day. Karen added to her comment about being undisciplined with the caveat, "But I tune in and ground myself often during the day."

Pam, seventy-four, spoke of washing dishes as a meditative practice. Another interviewee spoke of gardening as a time to "look behind what's obvious; look beyond what's immediately there." Others spoke of "clearing emotions" and "tuning in throughout the day" to get "realigned with Love and my mission to reflect love."

Women who have a *regular* practice of Self-Witnessing spoke most convincingly about feeling grounded and purposeful, calm, and coming from their best selves on a consistent basis.

Maddisen, sixty-one, is an example of a blended practice including solitude, spiritual practice, and working concretely with goals and plans. "I have a nonnegotiable one hour practice every day," she said. "In the morning I sit in my private space, meditate for twenty minutes, then answer ten dream questions if I've had a potent one." From there Maddisen reviews her "Ideal Scene Wheel" that we discussed as a check-in compass in the chapter Pioneering On, and sets an intention for the day.

However we engage the life-giving power of silence and solitude, the women I interviewed talked about its effects coming into play in everything they do: creative endeavors, work, caring for grand-children, being a rock-solid "go-to" person for others. It turns out to be a key differentiator between feeling a sense of stagnation and aimlessness versus feeling alive, strong, and consciously on the path of Further Becoming.

According to most of the 100 women, Self-Witnessing in Solitude and its associated practices bring guidance, affirmation, and direction; nonnegotiable for Pioneering On. I too trust what emerges in the quiet—sometimes just the assurance that, in the words of Norma, sixty-five, "I can feel that I'm part of something greater and always will be."

By investing time in purposeful solitude, we also model the counsel we long to give our younger sisters: Take time. Go in. Listen.

● *Story* ●

Sarah Delfont, sixty-two, almost didn't agree to an interview. Knee deep in policy writing for one of England's National Health System's charities and on self-titled "granny duty" her one day off, she wasn't sure she could be helpful to my collection of active-wisdom-in-motion. Ah…how wrong she was! Challenged by and passionate about bridging the huge gap between mainstream healthcare and the holistic world, Sarah is still at it with full vigor. As she also runs the health and well-being clinic pilot for oncology patients, seeing clients and facilitating groups, she still finds time to fulfill her role as trustee of a nonprofit in Tibet. A new grandchild and family members with disabling conditions don't make it easier. But Sarah isn't asking for easy.

I asked what her nonnegotiable practices were that help her do and be what she's doing and being right now.

"If I don't have enough solitude I can't do what I do," she answered. "Of course when it's chosen it's a luxury; when it's forced, it's torture. Years ago I would have thought that I'd find loneliness to be the biggest challenge at this time of my life. But no! In the last decade I've had to carve out time for solitude. I've always had the need for it—for the silence. And then the culture-driven fear comes on that speaks about the loneliness of old age.

"But we never talk about the solitude that is vibrant and enhances!" she continued. "I see friends in their eighties desperately trying to avoid solitude. To me it feels vital. It's very conscious. It helps me appreciate the minutiae of life and moments of just being. The smallest of things are so vivid. So I walk. I meditate. I cut out a lot of social things to find the balance."

Recently Sarah was called to support a family member caught in a crisis in India involving a mental institution, unfathomable bureaucracy, and a loved one in need. Gratefully it worked out well. With unassuming resilience and the backbone of a warrior, Sarah reflected, "What struck me more than anything was that in the chaos, the silence and moments of solitude are what sustained me."

QUOTES

"I crave solitude. Periods of solitude are where my biggest awakenings have happened. I built a log cabin on a knoll near the Blue Ridge Mountains and spent one week there almost every month for ten years. The practice of solitude is essential to my soul's well-being."

—MARCY W., SEVENTY-EIGHT

"I would say to women: go inside. Find quietness and peace within. Creativity seems to go hand in hand with spirituality, and spirituality goes hand in hand with time in solitude."

—ROBERTA E., SEVENTY-TWO

"I have found it incredibly helpful to have very strong inner practices. We need to be able to check in with ourselves, cultivate the ability to communicate with soul, and get clear guidance from the inside—not from the outside."

—LOIS S., FIFTY-FOUR

Antidote To

This Declaration is an antidote to the onslaught of noise from world news and from other people's opinions and influence. It's preventative to creeping suggestions of isolation, disempowerment, and the erosion of a noble place in the world. It's imperative as a way of feeding and fortifying our best selves; a bedrock of our continued becoming. We engage solitude to practice Self-Witnessing, then it begins to engage and transform us.

PRACTICE

An important part of starting or deepening any practice is the getting ready. Put another way, the biggest threat to enacting a new practice is making the goal too big at the start and then facing all the "little foxes" of resistance.

Identify a go-to place where you can easily shift into undistracted silence. It might be in your home—in a particular corner or window spot you enjoy. The chair should be comfortable and support the uniqueness of your body and how you like to sit. At this stage, we know what that is! You might have a view of trees, or the sky, potted flowers outside, or just the natural light that bathes your space. If the view inside your house brings more peace than the one outside, make sure it's free of clutter and has just the type of lighting you enjoy. Nearby, you have space for a hot drink or water and your book or journal. Create the type of space that welcomes you, where all the preparation is done and it sits waiting for nothing but you and the quiet.

If your "go-to" is outdoors, choose a place within ten minutes of your home if possible so there's no resistance about getting there. (Research shows we exercise more if the workout location is ten minutes or less away.) Know where to park ahead of time. Commit as much as possible to parking in the same place each time. Discover the path or general area that delights you, whether going to the right or left on the path. Since "hearing" beyond the senses requires a certain amount of relaxation, this will be different than finding a new rock face to scale or a particularly challenging hike to try. Consistency surrounding practice makes it more accessible and attractive to us.

Places for solitude are important. Start here. Have a go-to spot prepared; perfectly suited to you. It will beckon you to spend more time there. It will be your blank canvas for listening. Now you're ready.

TEND TO THE VESSEL WITH LOVE

We are learning to eat well, rest well, exercise well—with love.

Choices about coloring one's hair vs. going grey, wearing makeup or going natural, and getting "dressed" or not when heading out to the store on a Saturday vary across women age fifty and beyond. But the 100 women I interviewed definitely take their *health* and *wellness* seriously. Smart, loving care of ourselves is imperative for continuing to live vibrant lives and for filling whatever roles we choose in our families, our communities, and in the world.

Tending to the physical body—the vessel that is ours to manage and through which we express health, happiness, purpose—is another domain the 100 women spoke about when I asked what rituals, structures, and practices they enact that are nonnegotiable in their lives.

While the most frequent response to the above question was solitude/quiet time (including a variety of practices during)—numerically tied with relationships/connection to family and friends—the second most frequent response was taking good physical care of oneself.

HOW WE THINK ABOUT PHYSICAL SELF-CARE

Physical care practices fell into distinct categories. They were also talked about by many women as avenues for Further Becoming.

In other words, we don't just lift weights or practice yoga to add muscle mass or increase flexibility, though those outcomes are important. For most women I interviewed, the means or practice itself is a way we connect and express our best selves. The outcome is not primarily about looking a certain way, but about being able to do what we want in life and being who we want to be. We're empowered and enabled by how we feel about ourselves as wise disciplined women as well as by our strength and continued flexibility.

Joan Fisher, retired public school teacher and technology coordinator now in her early sixties, has battled weight issues all her life. She is currently on a steady diet of low carbs, fresh vegetables, and carefully chosen proteins. She is also going to the gym for the first time in her life. "I chose a gym where I don't have any pressure to wear those tight stretchy pants," she said. "I don't care how I look when I'm doing my workout. It's about how I feel… and let me tell you, when I leave that gym I feel alive and proud."

She continued, "My niece and nephews are everything, and I want to be here for them. I want them to see it's never too late to begin something new and take care of yourself with pride, at any age." She had lost seventy pounds so far. Her religious faith, she said, helped her stay the course.

The way we engage our physical practices when well over age fifty—Tending to the Vessel—has a quality of loving self-respect and self-appreciation. In the 100 interviews, women spoke about their nonnegotiable physical routines/habits as ways of honoring and guarding their worth. I love that. It's not out of fear or fragility, but from a desire to continue contributing, living, loving.

For Joan, her nonnegotiable practices started recently, after age sixty. For others, maintaining or increasing a healthy physical state has been going on much longer.

ENCOURAGING OUR SISTERS' EFFORTS

There certainly are women who hold the *desire* to become more balanced in their approach to Tending the Vessel, but aren't there yet. Desire is a good starting place.

Encouraging, supporting, and cheering each other on in these desires and endeavors is something we can do, sister to sister. Not as advice or as well-meaning nagging, but supporting good efforts we see other women already making or planning to make.

The reality is, we want advice only when we specifically ask for it! But witnessing and encouraging others' small efforts is huge, and contributes to the new ways women are banding together in solidarity toward further good in the world.

A woman in one of the virtual groups I was facilitating, though not a formal interviewee for this book, regularly shared her disappointment about not getting to the gym "like she should." We all listened and acknowledged her desire for more physical activity. One week, I asked her what she cherished most about the idea of going to the gym.

"It's really not the gym," she said. "It's that I want to feel myself active and free."

We asked what else "active and free" might look like for her. She immediately said, "Oh, walking in the woods near me!"

We then asked more questions: *what are the woods like? What kind of shoes would you wear to walk there? Are there particular clothes you like to wear when you walk there? What do you see in the woods?* At the end of this exploratory back and forth, completely free of judgment, pressure, "should" or shaming, she said, "I think I'll walk there twice this week. Can I check in with you all next week and let you know how I did?"

Over the next several weeks, she had taken long walks in the woods between one and four times each seven-day period. She discovered that though her left knee sometimes bothered her, she had far more stamina than she expected and could feel herself picking up the pace. More than that, she felt proud, bold, and full of self-respect.

And of course, *our* spirits were elevated, too. We all felt connected even more deeply from cheering her on.

THREE MOST DESIRED RESULTS

In the 100 interviews, I found three outcomes women collectively aim for in our nonnegotiable physical practices:

1. Flexibility
2. Energy
3. Strength

These are of no surprise to women in their fifties, sixties, seventies, and beyond who may already feel vibrant and active and want to stay that way. They may also prompt a helpful starting place—a loving nudge—for any of us who live in temporary miasma about starting a practice that may feel daunting.

On a trip to Spain in 2016 to facilitate a leadership retreat where we were co-located in a somewhat remote villa, I was able to observe each woman's (and man's) practices over the period of days we were working together.

One woman, Annika, in her late fifties rigorously skipped rope each morning, followed by a multi-mile run. I wouldn't go near either of those activities!—they are simply not right for me. But they certainly are for Annika. Another woman who normally cycles in the evening with her husband joined a thirty-minute yoga session outdoors at 7 a.m. with a colleague's video propped up on a folding chair.

I stayed with my own yoga stretch and aerobic routine privately in my room. In the evening, we all had the opportunity to walk the hilly neighborhood with the Mediterranean Sea in the viewing distance; a walk that felt good to us all.

SINKING TAP ROOTS OF DISCIPLINE

Skipping rope is probably not on many of our short lists for where we want to begin Tending the Vessel! The examples in Spain were more about activities modified to fit the setting we were in.

But there's something compelling about practices that are so regular in our lives that tap roots have been deeply sunk and are now part of the daily or weekly rhythm of our routine. Sinking tap roots means having such a regular practice that Tends to the Vessel that it shapes the continuous nature of how we feel, move, are. Women spoke in the 100 interviews about how disciplined practices make them feel empowered and alive. They create a distinct way of moving in the world when we've engaged the discipline to schedule and honor ourselves in this way. There's something about enacting a habit that creates presence and pride.

Beloved poet Mary Oliver said this:

> "The different and the novel are sweet, but regularity and repetition are also teachers…and if you have no ceremony, no habits, which may be opulent or may be simple but are exact and rigorous and familiar, how can you reach toward the actuality of faith, or even a moral life, except vaguely? The patterns of our lives reveal us. Our habits measure us. Our battles with our habits speak of dreams yet to become real."[12]

I love how she includes those of us who may battle with setting habits—and those for who some habits are still just dreams. Thank you, Mary, for naming that they are eventually "to become real."

Some women's physical practices are full on and structured. Some women need groups or classes as helpful motivation, especially for walking or yoga. Others I interviewed choose the quiet of their own homes for solo physical routines. Many cardio-type workouts necessitate going to the gym, though some women engage outdoor activities like golf, biking, hiking as their cardio routines.

---

12   Mary Oliver, *Long Life: Essays and Other Writings*, 2004 (Cambridge, MA: Da Capo Press, 2004).

Not surprisingly, our collective reverence for nature gives us a payoff physically as well as soulfully when exercise can come in that way. Walking in nature was mentioned so many times by the women I interviewed! It seems to feed our quest for solitude and loving care of the physical vessel.

YOGA

Without question and with statistically high saturation, yoga is what the 100 women over fifty, and especially in their sixties and seventies, reported as the biggest difference maker, satisfying the desire for flexibility, energy, and strength. I heard a wonderfully wide variety of descriptions about interviewees' yoga routines.

"Yoga and Pilates three times/week for flexibility and strength."

"At least twenty minutes of stretching, vinyasas, floor movements."

"Not power yoga but therapeutic yoga early every morning."

"My energy practice; movement in a ritual for eight minutes every day."

"As I do my yoga routine I'm asking to be opened, opened, opened; to move into love."

"When I travel I try to take my mat with me. If not, I do them on the hotel floor."

"Yoga is part of my devotional exercise daily."

"I salute the great rising sun as I begin my yoga and four-directions salute."

"I have a twenty- to thirty-minute routine of floor stretches, cat/cow, five sun salutations, vinyasa, and shivasina. Then I pray while on my back."

"I'm stiff unless I do my yoga stretches every morning."

"Kundalini yoga, especially when I'm confused."

"I hate warrior poses anymore and have learned to avoid them in classes. I do lots of power yoga otherwise."

"Stretch, stretch, stretch…yoga in the morning is a must."

CARDIO

One of the ways we as women are rewriting the narrative about life at this stage—particularly at sixty and later—is by not cozying up to a sedentary lifestyle. So often we have unconscious pictures of an "old person's lifestyle"—and it almost always involved lack of energy and something amiss when the bottoms of the feet hit the pavement. Wobbly. Unstable. But the women I interviewed and I want nothing to do with that, nor can we relate to it. Getting outdoors, making sure we're moving in energetic ways brings a sense of speed, strength, energy, and liveliness into our whole way of being.

And cardio activity is top of the list for this according to the 100 women.

Bonnie has practiced consistent and balanced self-care for many years. Now just shy of her sixtieth birthday she continues brisk walking every day, good eating, sound sleep, and regular stretching. The only thing missing was cardio.

After meeting with a personal trainer, Bonnie told me she realized that full on, heart-pumping activity was something she wanted to add to her routine "just to feel more fully alive." Twice a week she now works out on the elliptical machine at the gym where her son works. "I cannot believe how different I feel!" she said. "It really gives me more energy—in my attitude, too."

Many women also said they do both stretching routines/yoga routines and cardio workouts. The way the 100 women pursue cardio workouts, if at all, is quite individual.

The most common cardio activity mentioned was walking, followed by hiking (two women used the phrase "soft jogging"). Running, cross-country skiing, biking, dancing (movement to music, freeform dance, or classes), swimming, water exercise, working with a personal trainer, camping, and adventuring are all examples of the 100 women's cardio pursuits.

"I'm religious about it," said Ellie, sixty-one, about her morning nature walks with her dog Jackson. "My body has to be engaged!" "I have a quest for good health and vitality," said another at seventy-one.

Charlotte Tomaino, seventy, is author of *Awaking the Brain: the Neuropsychology of Grace* and director of Neuropsychology Services of Westchester. She offers thoughtful insight from years of working with clients who have brain injuries. An expert on the connection between neuroscience and spirit, Charlotte said, "It's important to manage our thinking on wellness issues—manage our thought-life around all the things related to health, aches, dementia, etc. They're very insidious. I specifically manage my thought-life so not to get caught in ageist thinking."

Charlotte has three areas of nonnegotiable practice in her life, each enacted with precision and rigor. "For Spirit, I practice love-appreciation, meditation, reflection, contemplation, and reading-listening." This reading and listening involves for Charlotte (and several other women I interviewed) reviewing a text three times from the Bible or other sacred writings and reflecting upon its meaning and inspiration each time.

"For the brain," Charlotte continued, "I practice love-appreciation, choosing my focus, regulating emotion, pursuing mastery/growth, productivity. And for the body I practice love-appreciation, water, nutrition, exercise, and sleep."

I was impressed to hear the way women like Charlotte spoke not only about what they do to Tend to the Vessel, but also how they *think* about it.

"*Lovingly* put your lotion on," said Lois, fifty-four, whose life-work has been rearranged around supporting women as shared in "Leaving Your Legacy," chapter 9. "Eat well. Get exercise. Pay attention to your needs. We can do small incremental practices. It depends on what each one may need. But pay attention to the relationship with the body. Take time to be with the body. And remember that small changes have a huge impact. Right now is the time. What we do really matters."

HEALTHY EATING

As Charlotte and Lois identified, healthy eating is another of the three major topics women mentioned across the board.

Eating in ways that suit our best selves is a path we often have to navigate by experimentation and information.

Where I live, there is an alternative diet or food path for every person who walks into Whole Foods Market! Finding one's practices related to food is a subject that's written about extensively by a wide range of authors and food gurus. In fact, Hay House announced recently that the number one selling book category right now is cookbooks!

Suffice it to say, women well over fifty are paying attention to themselves and to what facilitates flexibility, energy, and strength and staves off inertia, unwanted weight gain, and stiffness. That's not to say we are pressuring ourselves from external messages about how we should look or what we should fear. Rather, at its best it's a natural reflection of our love for our wholeness, perhaps for some the first time in quite this way. It's embracing our native state of grace, elegance, pacing, and poise.

The women I interviewed have taken note that high-calorie food, heavily processed food, sweets, and an overload of carbs do not pan out to support our best selves.

In my view, it's normal to like what's good for us. Many women find organically grown food to be their choice at this point. And of course, many cannot afford or choose not to afford it.

Hannah, fifty-eight, spoke in her interview from Germany about how in her late fifties she began approaching meals with a practice of "appreciative cooking," caring not only about the ingredients but the way she prepares them thoughtfully. Just the other day a colleague mentioned that she swears food tastes better when she has cooked it with love, as if it infuses the dish.

Susan Furness, fifty-eight, my friend and colleague in United Arab Emirates who is a thought partner and advisor to clients navigating communications in the digital age, said at age fifty-seven that she "grazes about seven times a day" rather than sitting down for discrete meals at traditional intervals. I do the same, which is easy because my office is in my home. If my children read this, they will be laughing that their mother dare write anything about cooking. Two days ago in a conversation with a new friend, he asked if I'm an "eat to live or live to eat person." I immediately said, "Oh…eat to live!" Since we are allowed to like some things and not like others without any guilt, I will happily say that I'm Done With cooking!

But enjoying a home-cooked dinner last week by a dear friend who is also a James Beard award-winning chef, I recognize how much I enjoy the artistry and skillful blending of ingredients to deliver unmistakably flavorful, healthy, and enjoyable meals. Though I'm not one to shop for such ingredients or spend any time studying them, thank heavens others are. I can enjoy the fruits of their labor.

Buying fresh, already-prepared proteins and mixing up side salads, completely satisfied at the four minutes of kitchen prep so I can get on with whatever I'm doing, is a perfectly acceptable way to eat well and Tend to the Vessel, too.

Not surprisingly, breakfast gets honorable mention by women as the most important fuel-inducing meal to start the day.

"I eat a good breakfast every day: poached eggs, greens, and berries—overall, a noninflammatory diet," Lois, age fifty-four, told me.

"What's most important to me now," said Marie W., seventy-seven, long-term powerhouse in the women's movement, "is to stay active and take care of my health so I can be active with my children and grandchildren and continue to contribute. They're my priority now. And we should be able to contribute throughout our entire lives. I mean, I don't want to raise flowers, I want to raise hell!"

We're all different in the way we see, buy, and eat food. But women over fifty seem largely the same in the overall theme of Tending to the Vessel with Love: eat well, cut-out carbs and sugar, go organic if possible, and drink lots of water.

We want ourselves and our sisters over fifty to do the same: to Take Care of the Vessel in whatever ways are loving and self-honoring—not to look a certain way, but to feel and be a certain way: flexible, energetic, strong, alive, and inwardly majestic.

REST AND SLEEP

Quite a few women I interviewed had to reschedule our morning phone appointments due to lack of adequate sleep. I recall emailing with Deborah, fifty-eight, on this subject the morning she had to reschedule.

"Sleep is everything," I'd said. To which she replied, "Isn't that the truth!"

I recall a wise elder telling me once that sleep is not as important as rest. At times when I've had trouble with sleep, I've found it helpful to rest nonetheless, and trust it will suffice. It has proven to be true.

Many women have relaxing rituals to begin the process of inviting a good sleep.

"I lie in bed and review three good things from that day," said one.

"I say a prayer about keeping my soul peaceful as I sleep," said another, "and I always feel the effect afterwards."

"I arrange to be in bed by 10 p.m. It has to be a very special event for me to stay out late and not make that bedtime. I set the alarm for eight and a half hours and almost always feel rested," said a third.

"I have a short ritual of taking off my makeup, washing my face, using toner and moisturizer, and putting on hand lotion. It's been a routine for so long my body recognizes the signal and begins to relax," said Sunny Kate, sixty-three, social worker and part-time business consultant to nonprofits. "No matter where I go, I take that ritual with me."

Though I've never taken to it myself, many women find that napping helps considerably. There is something about lying down and allowing the body to completely relax into a brief restorative nap. The day I wrote this short inclusion about napping, Arianna Huffington, whose brainchild The Huffington Post Media Group I had the pleasure of conducting Conscious Business workshops in, posted on LinkedIn: "If you love someone, let them nap." Her book *The Sleep Revolution: Transforming Your Life, One Night at a Time* is a best seller for a reason.

When it comes to napping, rest is the aim, and sleep is optional.

HEALTH PRACTITIONERS

Perhaps because I did not specifically ask, the women I interviewed did not talk about the health practitioners they engage or how often they do so. Women with financial constraints mentioned how paying for eventual health needs poses a worry. Others mentioned the importance of planning wisely for long-term care, especially as a piece of advice they would give our younger sisters.

Because women have been acculturated to think of themselves last after thinking/caring for others, it seems important to say as relates to Tending to the Vessel with Love: we should all have a practitioner or network of practitioners in whatever our care tradition is to whom we can turn for care. Having a relationship with a trusted care practitioner ahead of any emergency saves tremendous anxiety when/if an urgent need arises.

Tending the Vessel with Love is a way we tend our worthiness and value. There is something delicious, soothing, and fortifying about having practices for which we've sunk tap roots because we love how they make us feel and we love the effects they bring continuously.

How we think about and talk about the body, especially after our mid-fifties in a culture where ageism is present in entrapping and hypnotic ways, should be an important part of our Further Becoming. Rather than an object of woe or a symbol of decline, we can claim our body vessels as a practice field for continual renewal. Wise women make a concerted effort to be its master.

● *Story* ●

Betsy Fuller, seventy-four, never had a traditional life. Raised by liberal parents in the South, graduating from Duke University, embarking upon the "grand adventure" of teaching, youth ministry, and one year of seminary, studying Greek (of all things!), then finding herself with the need to earn as a divorced mother of two, Betsy persevered. A foray into the insurance industry as a training developer, then work in an entirely different field: the Council on Aging. Betsy directed Older Americans Act services like Meals on Wheels and eventually became deputy of Senior and Long-Term Care Services at South Carolina Department of Health & Human Services (HHS) system. (Think government.)

Overseeing 600 workers and eight regional administrators in various programs, at age sixty-nine, her appreciative manager asked her the magic question one day. "What would you really like to do at this point?"

Four years before this question was asked, Betsy had discovered yoga at age sixty-five. "I think of this as a symbol for all women: that I started taking yoga at sixty-five," she said. "I did it to protect my health and body and mind. I never dreamed that I could bend my body like this! Yoga and meditation are nonnegotiable," to which she added, "as are walking and a good sense of humor."

Betsy then became a certified yoga instructor and massage therapist while still working at HHS. All of this is to say, when her manager asked Betsy what she'd really like to being doing, Betsy was prepared. She immediately answered that she'd like to implement a leadership program that reduced stress. And that is how she negotiated a new job description centered around mindfulness practices for HHS employees.

In a short while, Betsy introduced a modified mindfulness program based on Jon Kabat-Zinn's internationally recognized Mindfulness Based Stress Reduction practices (MDSR) across forty-six counties, including supervisors and employees. She writes a weekly wellness newsletter which includes mindful eating, emotional maturity, listening, and self-awareness. Supervisors were all supplied yoga mats—in a government agency! (Let that sink in.)

Betsy is still at it. "There's much more gentleness in the collective environment now," she reported. "I hear people counsel each other, 'Just take a deep breath.'"

"Life just gets better," she added. "Every decade has been better than the last."

Clearly, Betsy's uptake of Tending the Vessel in her own life had a ripple effect outward on many other lives. We never know what our love-impelled practices might inspire in others, too.

QUOTES

"First is nutrition: my diet has been full of nutrients since my thirties. Every morning I have a healthy smoothie or juice drink. I make sure to get enough sleep. I do early morning therapeutic yoga—not power yoga— and once a month I take a Qui Gong class. I do my own Qui Gong one to two times a week. I'd say to other women: 'Never stop moving.'"

ANNIE B., SIXTY-ONE

"Wellness is crucial! I do yoga, meditate, practice Hindu breathing, and drink lots of water. I work out three days/week doing Pilates or tai chi. And I do my spiritual path. I have to do these things. I have to be well."

—CAROLE J., EIGHTY

"I start with a clean diet: simple foods, organic labeling. I buy humanely sourced meat. Exercise for me is critical: stretches, walking, and biking every day to get the blood moving. And I do my best to stay in prayer/mindful observation all day."

—CINDY W., SIXTY

Antidote To

This Declaration is an antidote to creeping inertia and the unconscious submission to age-related decline. Simple routines of loving self-care that feel good (rather than pressured or punitive) build new pathways of empowerment. Every effort makes a difference.

PRACTICE

Tomes have been written and libraries filled with books on every topic touched upon in this chapter: nutrition, sleep, good exercise. I am choosing to focus on yoga, one practice that the women I interviewed love and find undeniably beneficial. Of course, in addition to yoga it's recommended to eat well, sleep well, and get aerobic exercise, too.

If you have not tried simple yoga yet or don't trust your practice as masterful enough to do alone at home in a way that supports good alignment and safe postures, ask a few friends for local studio recommendations. Call the studio(s) that appeal. Ask about free drop-in classes for a beginning student. Choose an entry level class that's a good day/time for you. Go. Don't worry about the clothes you wear (yoga does not require matching colors with cute cut-outs). Wear two pieces that allow free movement as your body warms up (think sleeveless) and a good support bra. That's all you need.

If you have the discipline and space to practice yoga at home and a basic routine that works for you, get a mat. A mat rolled out signals the practice space (literally) and the start of your practice time. Identify exactly where you will keep it for easy retrieval, and the exact space where you'll roll it out in your home. Think in terms of three mornings per week if you're starting a home routine. Create a routine that works for you that's at least ten minutes. (Mine is a series of simple floor stretches on my back, ten cat/cow, five sun salutation vinyasas with cobra pose and downward dog, three boat poses for the core, and a shavasana.)

Some women are motivated by joining a regular class. Prepaying for a class of six sessions or so is a sure way to make yoga a routine and get the benefit of others' energy and of trained instruction. You may want to do a combination of the above—two classes/week, two practice sessions at home/week.

Having a system in place—either starting as a new learner in a class, setting up a routine space at home, or joining a prepaid regular class—invites us to enact a yoga practice and stave off self-defeating voices that say it's too hard or too much of an investment. As vessels of active wisdom, we know exactly how to set ourselves up for gentle success.

DECLARATION 7

INHABIT BEAUTY

We are learning to be enveloped by the beauty we see and are, without and within.

Out on the water in my kayak yesterday, the setting sun delivered a personal Monet across the ripples, a blue/gold watercolor without the painter present. I marveled at how beauty is an expression of limitless Soul, a political act without trying to be. My day had included many intense work hours, a canceled dinner which brought a brief bout of loneliness, and some unimaginable national news involving the separation of children and their parents. As my kayak bobbed on the evening ripples, I sunk into "peace…which passeth understanding";[13] the presence of such profound satisfaction that it caused my breathing to downshift. *This is why I came here*, I thought.

"Enough is a feast," it is written. Can we ever get enough of beauty?

---

13 The Bible, King James Version, Philippians 4:7.

With all the false narratives on what beauty is and what we must do to buy it and apply it, we as women over fifty have emerged at least somewhat above the culture-based fog to find ourselves attracted to a purer form of beauty. This attraction defines a piece of who we are at this stage. As it turns out, we must have it in our lives.

AN EXPANDED DEFINITION

"I find beauty in simple things and experiences," said Beth, seventy. "For example, having flowers around is a practice. Watching a bud on my hibiscus plant grow from day to day, then burst into such vibrancy and determination. And in a different way, waving to the garbage men as they work through my street, hoping they receive my small token of appreciation for making life livable. Or taking pleasure from the lively greeting the four-year-old next door gives me when we happen into our front yards together."

For Sunny, sixty-three, beauty in her home is "something I have to have." "My home is my respite," she explained. "It has served me and saved me. What I see outside and what my eyes rest on inside is really important. Even walking out to my cul-de-sac and seeing the circle of neighbors, each one expressing their own sense of home—the blinds up and someone placing a plant in the window, or my other neighbor with lights in their tree—it's very alive. The scene changes every day. Beauty is part of that."

"I have a chair that faces my garden," Christina said at seventy. "I write from that place. I think from that place."

Katie, age fifty-five, said, "I have to live where I can see the ocean from my window. Where we are now was part of the beauty and peace I envisioned: where the land meets the sea. I'm surrounded by natural beauty. I don't take that for granted."

Beauty in our home space is one arena where we breathe it in, letting it surround us, soothe us, happify us. And why not? Women innately understand beauty as part of the ever-unfolding expression of life—as a language unto itself.

Perhaps we love the language of beauty because it doesn't interpret or need to be interpreted. It doesn't exert. It neither overdoes nor underdoes. It just is. Right now I glance out my dining room window at the beautiful, tall hibiscus bush I planted in my son's name. It's bursting with blue flowers. I can't not see it. A double-negative, I know, but it isn't quite accurate to say, "I have to see it." I don't. Some days, perhaps I wouldn't, or not in this way. But today as I hold him in my thought and glance out the window, its beauty is so there I can't not see it. And I see Sam, and love, at the same time.

WORDLESS LANGUAGE

It was satisfyingly surprising to discover the importance of quiet and solitude in the lives of the 100 women I interviewed—hence the birthing of chapter 5, "Self-Witnessing in Solitude."

Not surprising then is its second cousin, Beauty.

The relevance and recognition of beauty's place in the age of active wisdom appears with the soothing absence of voices or commentary. When women spoke about it, it had an almost stammering simplicity to it…almost wordless, expressed more with sighs and awe. I reached out to a handful of women who spoke of beauty with this simple genuineness because I wanted to hear more.

"Beauty doesn't feel separate any longer," said Cristine Milton, sixty-eight, retired professor of cultural anthropology who now shares her passion for people and places via writing, photography, and leading custom travel experiences. "It's in me, of me, outside of me. It just "is" and I flow with it all the time. It is actually the unbeautiful that catches my attention now, so unusual that seems."

Cristine recalled a moment in Ethiopia several years earlier. "It was a time of part sunset, part blue hour, when all of the colors of the sky were not only broadcast throughout the sky, but were radiating upward from the earth also. Smoke began wafting from thatched-roof chimneys, livestock were being penned for the night, children did their last scramble indoors. Earth and sky were truly locked in embrace—an orange, gold, purple, dusky embrace—and I drove through it for almost an hour, the brush and soil glowing. Time was suspended, which is perhaps why I am able to return to that feeling and sense of beauty so easily and why it dwells in me. It was an external beauty, not of my making, not from within me. Yet it embedded itself in me and has been my calming point ever since. So beauty is a feeling, a full sensory explosion of tranquility, vastness, and color."

Travel is for some of us a way we find our visual worlds shaken up and new shapes, configurations, unexpected symbols, or occurrences of beauty delivered.

Two women I interviewed have taken up professional photography as a result of the astounding scenes they beheld and could find no expression for other than through a camera lens. The exposure to different permutations of beauty enlarges our capacity to hold them, and as a result our inner capacity for beauty is enhanced.

Indeed, external scenes or sounds of beauty are for many women blended with the internal capacity to translate and incorporate them without efforting the process, as Cristine described.

Mary Hostetter, fifty-four, a realtor, business owner, and founder of a popular blog on conscious homes spoke similarly about the role of beauty in her life. "To me it shows the exquisiteness of the universe and how we are parts of the whole," she shared.

Marie P., fifty-five, said it this way: "Noticing what is right there almost all of the time—life's preciousness—it's everywhere if I can stop and savor it. It causes me to get out of my head. I often feel teary and deeply grateful."

It seems the relief beauty gives us provides natural balance to the wearing of the world.

MUSIC

Music is another form of beauty women over fifty wrap ourselves in, allowing it to transport us to places without the accompaniment of human voices and the noise of opinions. The up-swells, gentle cadences, or trumpeting triumphs of a symphonic piece performed at Chautauqua's Performance Hall where I live, with its open-air performance pavilion allowing gentle breezes to drift through, deliver a beauty that surpasses anything social media or socializing could ever rival.

Hearing music, dancing to music, making music, and singing all fit within the theme of Inhabiting Beauty in the age of active wisdom.

A European colleague and friend just turned sixty. She had an epiphany about how her work hours as a consultant crowded out any possible time to do what she had always loved: singing. She'd been in a choir nearly two decades ago and missed it terribly. The desire had been calling to her for years. At a women's retreat to work on refreshing her life goals and purpose, she proclaimed a commitment to return to choir singing. In less than six months she found a masterful men and women's choir who happily accepted her. Since then, she changed her job to create more balance and has been touring Europe on performance with the choir, singing her heart out. She declared, "It's one of the things I most love to do."

When the beauty of music resides within us, it's an irrepressible influence—whether we're creating it or seeking to be one of its enthusiastic fans.

VISUAL ART

How often I heard women in the 100 interviews speak of taking up painting!

My own mother picked up oil painting in her seventies. She then started an amateur photography interest in order to take pictures, then use the images as the base outline for her paintings.

In Houston recently, I was taken to a studio that features a private line of clothing. The woman who greeted Kelly and I was stunningly beautiful in her classic black haute couture outfit and subtly coiffed hairstyle. Quintessentially Texas in her elegance and style, she provided us a walk-through, then left us to ourselves. At the end of our visit, Kelly mentioned the book I was writing. In turn, I shared how much beauty and creativity becomes fertile and irresistible to many of us in our fifties, sixties, seventies, eighties.

"Oh," she exclaimed, her eyes sparkling and her body language loosening into spontaneous movement and energy. "I just started painting!" she said. "I go out in my garage and just get lost in painting. I love it! I love the colors and the feeling. I'm even thinking that someday I might enter an exhibit."

What I found so intriguing was how her own beauty changed when she talked about beauty. Her presentation was stunning to begin with; a model of stately womanhood. But when she spoke about painting! Her face lit up and there was a childlike aliveness that made her whole presence radiate. I wouldn't have missed it for the world, and I told her how sparkling she became when she talked about painting. You can believe how ardently I cheered her new endeavor, too…though her attraction to it was irrepressible no matter what anyone thinks!

Photography.

Drawing.

Painting.

There may be delight in the outcomes, for sure…but there seems a distinct delight even more so in the dabbling, literally and figuratively.

Having given up perfectionism as a Done With That, we have taken up the perfectly imperfect marks of our own budding art strokes, like the spontaneous sunsets reflected on water around and underneath my kayak. We engage the colors and deepen our relationship with them while painting. We discover how they respond to intense vs. light marks with the brush—and how we do, too.

I read an ad recently for a women's creativity retreat. It offered a wide range of activities from beading to painting to woodwork to collage in small cabins scattered across a mountain setting. I love what it said about the retreat's aim: "Come away and create with no deadline, and no pressure to produce. Come to simply enjoy the process."

This is what captures our relationship to beauty at this stage. Our aesthetic eye and love of beauty is more about noticing it and engaging with it than about creating anything for consumption.

Cindy W. said at age sixty, "I need to see and practice beauty. I have a watercolor practice. I use a coloring book at times. And I take regular trips to the ocean. I've started collecting seashells! I focus on things that bring hope, and beauty is one of them. Music, art, good news stories. I want to amplify the beautiful, the noble."

Photographer Cristine, sixty-eight, spoke of merging what she finds beautiful in her own consciousness with what's eye-catching in parts of the developing world where she frequently travels. "If I want more beauty in my experience, I may write or work on my photos. Beauty can be laying two photos on top of each other and turning them into one," she said.

For every woman there is a unique engagement with whatever colors, enriches, swaths, and enlivens our souls. How much we all need that! Beauty helps us remember what is good. It helps remind us what is eternal.

HOPE IN BEAUTY/BEAUTY IN HOPE

Beauty helps us do what Martie, seventy-three, does as a practice: "choosing hope over despair."

The presence of beauty in our lives and our growing capacity to notice it and spend time enjoying it does, it seems, bring us hope.

Pam, seventy-four, lost a child years ago—a life experience most would agree is the most difficult of all. Finding one's way back—finding hope—is not necessarily a given. It takes grace. Resilience in the face of endless grief. One foot in front of another.

Pam told me she discovered that "Beauty is a way of saying Yes! to life. No matter the hurt or pain, there is beauty somewhere, within or without, to nourish my soul and create a bridge toward acceptance."

If beauty is a recipe for resilience and healing, let us welcome it.

Women indeed spoke of the beauty of the human spirit; hope inducing and hope confirming. One mentioned seeing beauty in the courage of other women when they take steps to stand in their truth. Another spoke of "the beauty of human striving to be excellent and good." She went on to say, "And human kindness is oh, so beautiful too."

A neighbor I know well, seventy, told me of visiting the famous Red Rocks outdoor theatre several years ago at age sixty-eight. Ten thousand seats stack high over a stage between massive boulders in geology's fountain formations dating back to the Jurassic period. The best musicians in the world perform there; on a clear night one can not only hear Yo-Yo Ma or Van Halen, but gaze upward at the sparkling heavens and a full view of fields for miles.

The night Gloria and her friend attended, though, wasn't starry. Although Red Rocks has a policy of smart weather planning, the heavens broke open unexpectedly. Gloria recalled quickly getting soaked by the downpour. "I was so ticked; it felt like such a loss all around." But then Gloria felt something land on her lap.

"The guy next to me had given me a large blue poncho—and one for my friend too," she said. "The rain was so loud and everyone was scurrying I almost couldn't hear the words he was shouting. 'My wife and I always bring two extras!' he yelled. Then off they ran. Everything rearranged. All of a sudden I loved being there. I loved the rain. I loved the fun mess we were in."

Says poet Rainer Maria Rilke:

Ahead Of All Parting

Ah, not to be cut off,
not through the slightest partition
shut out from the law of the stars.
The inner—what is it?
if not intensified sky,
hurled through with birds and deep
with the wings of homecoming[14]

PERSONAL BEAUTY

Indeed, not only are we not "shut out from the law of the stars" but we seem to feel closer and more intimate in our relationship to beauty as years increase.

How do we engage the full spectrum of beauty and color? How does it manifest personally when our own outward color may be physically fading?

The women I interviewed had a wide range of perspectives on how they engage the notion of personal beauty at this stage. Several spoke of feeling more beautiful than ever before. I attribute this

---

14   Rainer Maria Rilke, "Ahead of All Parting," in *The Selected Poetry and Prose of Rainer Maria Rilke*, 1995 (New York: Random House, 1995).

to the ownership women have for who they are internally, alongside not worrying about what others think or being motivated by pleasing others.

Many have happily let go of any quest to keep the body in exactly the same shape as in younger years, though still committed to Tending the Vessel with Love in the best and healthiest way for this stage. "I've made peace with the changes of my body," said Cindy. "I don't freak about it." At the same time, she is diligent about disciplined and loving care of herself and what she has.

Our hair seems to be another canvas upon which we create whatever we want in order to claim our creative expression of self.

"I'll color my hair 'til the day I die," said a fifty-nine-year-old interviewee who lives in LA and asked not to be named. "Aging here is not for the faint of heart!"

"I stopped coloring my hair twenty years ago," said Carol Miyagishima, sixty-five, former director of Chancellor's Leadership Studies Program at a prominent university in Colorado and a specialist on race, class, and gender. "My students loved it. They encouraged me. They said, 'That's exactly what I'm going to do when I'm older!'"

"I'm experimenting with the grey thing," said Cheryl, my sixty-seven-year-old colleague who lives in the southwest US. "I'm letting it come in. Then I'll see if I like it and what I want to do next."

In tributes to the late Barbara Bush, her silvery hair was mentioned as a marker of her strength and authenticity. She dared to be exactly who she was and say exactly what she thought. Her bold willingness to be herself, including proudly wearing a silvery-grey mane, was a characteristic both loved and lauded.

Of course, our hair is not the only personal canvas on which we express ourselves.

"I try my best to value my outside beauty and take care to be well groomed, wear makeup, and flattering clothes, and more importantly to work very hard at expressing myself in ways that engage others in a heartfelt way that brings out their beauty. The Native American concept of 'walking in beauty' says it best for me: not just my outer appearance but noticing the light in others, their inner and outer beauty; being a good steward to the earth to sustain her beauty; honoring others," said Katie from far west Washington state.

"Wrinkles matter far less than I thought they might," said Cristine. "A scarf can be the greatest accessory I own now."

The beatific expression of our Further Becoming is something about which we seem to have growing appreciation and reverence. It's no longer primarily about how we personally/physically show up in the world, at least not from a socially pressured perspective. It's more the recognition of where we belong: in beauty, surrounded by it, creating it, and basking in it.

The luxury of beauty—painting it, needlepointing it, drawing it, coloring it, kayaking in it, walking through it, listening to it, noticing it, writing it—is both external and internal. We recognize somehow that we are not separate from it; we can be immersed in it and express beauty as we see it.

How profound that the very stage where we are made to believe beauty fades, it actually comes online more fully in a purer form.

I find it a relief that no matter how demanding my writing has been on a given day or how intense my efforts to deliver the best service to coaching clients, I can launch my kayak on the shores of Dream Cove at 6 p.m. on another summer eve and have an experience with living beauty every time. The particular ducks that appear (one quacking yesterday as I paddled behind her—was she leading me? warning me?). Whether a black and white loon will suddenly pop up from his fishing expedition while the light shifts where I'm rowing. These moments of wonder subsume the conundrums I may have been contemplating a short while ago.

The fact that beauty continues to introduce its loveliness and awe gives us not only hope, but the conviction that another influence is greater and present, and we can access it. Perhaps that's because we recognize now it was never something to manufacture or feel pressured about. Beauty is something we deserve. At this stage of life, we are meant to slow down and appreciate it, cloak ourselves in it, and recognize that we reflect it.

◉ *Story* ◉

I met Heather Starsong when she was eighty-one years old. Her name is a wonderful reflection of her: with an unmistakable sparkle in her eyes, a knowing presence, silver hair perfectly becoming to her delicate features, and strength in her gaze that transmits how straight on she sees things while still carrying dancer-like beauty and grace. She described herself as "mostly retired" but still doing Rolfing® (a trademarked form of hands-on physical therapy for structural integration) with clients. After twenty-seven years of being single, she'd also just remarried.

Heather was once an elementary school teacher and also a dance teacher. As a dancer and sensitive to movement and flow, Heather eventually studied Rolfing® and was on the faculty at the Rolf Institute for sixteen years. She spoke about her life as having three themes: a career of bodywork; marriage, children and learning; and a spiritual path that started with agnostic parents, attendance at various local churches, becoming a devout Presbyterian, taking in yoga and Quakerism for a while, "exploring woo-woo," as she put it, and then a Shamanic path. Fifteen years ago she "dropped into Buddhism."

Heather was working on her third novel when we spoke. But it wasn't the book she wanted to talk about. It was the beauty in her life and her new relationship to it.

"I was what people would say was pretty. I spent a lot of time with it and am still a good-looking woman, but I gave up all the focus on 'what shall I wear?' That was a huge shift. I'm happier now letting go of all of the drama. Things don't torment me anymore."

Heather found herself unexpectedly moved recently while watching her grandchildren leap and dance. She thought, 'I used to do that!' Though not leaping anymore, per se, she still goes out in nature and enjoys hikes in the midst of all the beauty. "The call of the light—the way the light looks on the maple trees—the waves—my love of my children—I'm here between two worlds. There is happiness and poignancy and peace now. That's important."

In recent years, Heather made a decision to explore the question of what it's like to give unconditional love and to see beauty everywhere. She decided to "lavish attention" on it. Then this past January she met Clay. He was a volunteer driver for medical appointments and took her to her follow-up. They reconnected shortly afterwards with a walk, then got together once a week, and then on a hike one day decided to cohabitate. "We give each other a lot of space. It's very gentle," she said. "We've decided to get married because we want the witnessing of community. I am quite, to my surprise, in love and about to get married to a truly fine man."

As an octogenarian, Heather is a writer, storyteller, hiker, dancer, Rolfer®, lover of beauty, and now newly married. Continuing to focus on "learning to love better; being love," Heather reported finding beauty in everything.

QUOTES

"Being able to recognize the simplicity and beauty of what blessings really are helps me to untangle when I'm getting too complicated."

—NORMA J., SIXTY-FIVE

"It's a beautiful journey. Despite the challenging era we're in, future people are going to say women really did make change. Life really is abundant. How blessed we are. In reality, it is all a gift."

—CAROL K., SEVENTY

"How powerful attention is. We can choose where to give it. My grandmother used to tell me that when you die, you go to an island of your heart where your memories are stored. So memorize good things."

—DAWNA M., SEVENTY-FIVE

"There's a traditional Japanese kabuki lion dance. One interpretation portrays a wise elder with white hair in the father image in a white kimono. A young man in the son image comes out in a red kimono, symbolizing the impulsiveness of youth. They do a dance together which is intricate. This kind of imagery with the colors and symbolism conveys something words can't. I find so much beauty in this cycle of life message and how it's artistically represented."

—CAROL M., SIXTY-FIVE

Antidote To

This Declaration is an ode to what women naturally carry within us no matter how patriarchal powers have tried to appropriate the concept of beauty for exportation, production, and gain. To see beauty we must be beauty. Surrounding ourselves with a cloak of beauty is a tremendous act of soft power, rich with color, elegance, and diversity. We deserve it.

PRACTICE

It matters not if we choose to create beauty, engage with beauty through music or art, or immerse ourselves in nature's beauty. What matters is that we develop easy access to it.

Choose your favorite way to relate to beauty. It should be something that absolutely delights you! When you think of it, relaxation and pleasure spontaneously arrive.

It may be classical music; a particular composer. It may be a potted plant with feminine leaves, wanting to grace a corner in your room. It may be a palette of watercolors and a brush, wanting your composing marks on a waiting canvas of your favorite size. It might be a path you think about near your home but rarely walk.

Is there a container garden to plant? A flowering shrub wanting to fill in the space outside your window? Have you put sewing or needlepoint aside for too long? Or singing, drumming, piano lessons?

Choose the one that calls you most, to which you have easy access, perhaps with just a little effort that feels fun and flirtatious.

Now, take the first step to engage it.

What did you reach for? How did the beauty within you leap?

CREATE A MOAI

*We are learning to find sisterhoods
where we can be witnessed,
celebrated, and witness others.*

In response to the question *"What's most important in your life right now?"* the women I interviewed most frequently said "family/ relationships" along with "inner/spiritual growth." These two categories have top billing in terms of importance.

The definition of family/relationships is different for each woman, of course. Some women were specific about relationships with their adult children. Grandchildren were frequently mentioned as a special category unto itself, usually part and parcel of being in relationship with adult children. (Grandparenting is covered in chapter 9, "Leaving Your Legacy.")

But almost across the board, whether interviewees were grandparents or parents, single or married, *female friendships* were reported as a major source of fulfillment, affirmation, and inspiration for women over age fifty, especially for those in their sixties and seventies. We are learning not only the sweetness of these friendships but their life-giving properties as part of the blueprint of what makes a rich life.

How we've come to this learning is not the way those who grew up in "Blue Zones"[15] have learned it and lived it, however. Blue Zones are areas in the world where research shows people live the longest with the highest happiness quotients. A central characteristic in Blue Zones is belonging to a "moai" of some sort—the Japanese word for small, close-knit groups who remain connected from childhood to elderhood. Not surprisingly, the 100 women I interviewed find profound affirmation and nourishment in moais or sisterhoods with other women. As mentioned in chapter 3, "Done With That," this theme is directly related to a desire for exothermic (invigorating) relationships and a Done-With-That stance on endothermic (draining) relationships.

Blue Zone research also identifies two features of one's social life as strong predictors of how happy one is, further connected to how long one will live.

One feature is related to the presence of close friends. Close friends are defined as people you can call if you need money (in other words, with whom you can be vulnerable and needy) and who you could call if you were in an existential crisis or in need of an emergency ride to the hospital.

The second feature is called social integration: how many people you talk to each day, whether weak bonds (the barista serving your coffee) or strong bonds (your best friend).

---

15 Dan Buettner, *The Blues Zones of Happiness: Lessons from the World's Happiest People* (Washington, DC: National Geographic Partners, 2017).

The moais or sisterhoods I have in my own experience, and those talked about by some of the 100 women I interviewed, fit these essential categories. For other women, close social relationships are satisfied through family ties.

About family ties, we all know of family relationships that have not produced environments of understanding, acceptance, love. What a good thing it is, then, to be able to "choose one's family" as the saying goes! Sisterhood—as well as motherhood, fatherhood, daughterhood, etc.—might be found where we didn't expect it after discovering its void where we did. It's proof that the qualities resonant in sweetly nourishing relationships—proven to make us happier and live longer—can be found wherever we are and whoever we are. I certainly know this from my own experience.

Some women consider sisterhoods in structured groups to which they belong part of their spiritual practice. Women who attend regular get-togethers in "deep spiritual friendships" consider it a form of practice because of the powerful insights they gain and how it changes them in meaningful ways. These insights are gained not from well-meaning (but unhelpful) advice or opinions, but from the spaciousness of thoughtful listening and acknowledgment. The environments of these regular get-togethers invite each woman's wisdom and ongoing learning to be expressed—in relation to herself and in relation to unfolding life events. The learning is supported and expanded by the seasoning of others' experiences and perspectives.

Janice, fifty-eight, spoke in her interview about the role of a moai in her life. "I'm in a circle of women who are absolutely amazing. Every Saturday we have breakfast, do a run, and then share our experiences. We've been meeting for eight years. We're truth-tellers—we help each other think things through. When we talk about real life in such an honest way, it's magic."

Janice's moai came about organically. It obviously includes a shared physical activity. Indeed, many of the moais studied in Blue Zones include walking and talking and/or a community meal on a regular basis as part of the moai's DNA. For some women, the inclusion of a non-stressful physical activity like walking is a welcome part of the connecting ritual.

"I walk one to three times a week with other women," said another Brenda I interviewed in her mid-fifties. "We've been doing it for thirteen years! I'm closer to them than my own sister. We run things by each other, exchange parenting advice, discuss work and other things. They are like family."

Women describe these sisterhoods as hugely important to their happiness, discovering them as places where, in the words of one woman, "I'm met right where I am and can be exactly who I am."

Imperfection, vulnerability, and insights-in-process are all seen as contributions, not weaknesses. They allow everyone to relax. They allow social masks to be doffed and mutual exploration to take place. As we've all experienced at one time or another, this kind of environment builds bonds of trust and acceptance that fortify us, even between get-togethers. And women who don't have opportunities to cultivate circles of sisterhood mentioned it as a distinct void in their lives.

Leandra, seventy-one, is an example of participation in a moai with a different kind of origin and structure than Janice's or Brenda's. "I've been in a women's group for five years," Leandra said. "It's four of us. We study readings, poems; talk about what they've meant to us. Then we ask, 'What's going on in your life? How can I help?' We're very different women. Being able to feel like I've gone into the hearts and minds of other women—and to validate what's going on inside me—to grow into what I'm meant to be rather than coming from fear-based old ways—is a wonderful gift." (After Leandra divorced and moved to Kentucky, as described in chapter 1, "Pioneer On," she reported that this same circle of women continued to meet using FaceTime.)

Gael, sixty-two, described something similar though the origins of friendship were already established. "My close loving friendships over thirty years have deep roots," she said. "We review the last week with each other every week. They have helped me love myself through the stuff that I didn't handle well. These relationships—well, they are nonnegotiable."

WHY MOAIS DESERVE A CLOSER LOOK

As mentioned in chapter 3, "Done With That," many women over fifty speak of having little time or tolerance for superficial socializing anymore. But while shifting away from conversation that feels empty or shallow, we are also finding ourselves leaning toward the types of exothermic connections that moais deliver.

I love what one woman said. "I find women at this age so generous!" I know I did when conducting these interviews. She described spending exothermic time with friends as a new ritual. "I would say to other women, 'Who are you connected to deeply?' Pursue those relationships. It has saved me."

In my research I learned that moais don't require origination from a young age or even similar backgrounds and interests. So what do they require?

- Regular committed time with each other; not occasional or happenstance but pre-planned and honored.

- A shared purpose/focus.
- A simple process including timekeeping and a facilitator or rotating host who guards the process. The process may include a reading, response to the reading, a focus question, or a predetermined topic.
- The spirit of reciprocity. Each participant has equal time and is committed to generous listening as much as to speaking.

As this recipe gets repeated, women over fifty find these spaces for uninterrupted speaking and nonjudgmental listening a precious commodity. To hear and be heard; to be acknowledged and affirmed; to be witnessed without fixing is indeed a gift.

"Joining is not my thing usually," said Annette at sixty-two. "But I joined a philanthropic organization and the sisterhood is tremendous."

Annette also participated in a six-month moai pilot group I held early in 2018. I named the focus Reflecting on Purpose. We met every three weeks with a simple process I offered from my years of facilitating moais. Five women between ages fifty-five and sixty-four had equally allotted time to use in whatever way we wished related to how we're currently engaging purpose and how it's playing out in our lives, decisions, observations.

Each participant was asked to make a commitment to be present every three weeks for ninety minutes. We agreed on confidentiality and other norms, and I acted as a light facilitator—usually important at the start of a new group.

After six months, one participant wrote, "This group has become part of my soul's DNA. I have been heard, witnessed, and valued. That led to me publishing an article, securing two book reviews for publication, and taking a leadership role in co-editing a book. I've also begun to speak up more at meetings. How remarkable to hear someone distill in a beautiful accurate way what you hear, witness, what strikes you. For the first time I feel I have been heard. It's surprising how many people and groups want to tell you how to fix their problems—but this group has showed me another way to witness."

At this stage in the age of active wisdom, many of us have grown tired of others delivering answers or suggesting fixes to the interlaced wonders and complexities of our lives. We want to hear ourselves and be encouraged to tap our own knowing which is often drowned out by noise around us or even within us.

Though able facilitation can help greatly, it is certainly not required.

In the two moais of which I'm a part, we are all leaderful in the sense of timing ourselves and being true to the same process each time. Both groups meet by phone; something I learned has just as much efficacy as meeting in person. We're each experienced in the dynamics of group discussion and feedback, which helps.

I believe we can all learn these skills even if we don't feel grounded in them yet. The importance of having these deep connections makes it worthwhile to try.

One of the moais to which I belong has given me support and motivation to keep writing this book; a daunting task at times as I've felt the responsibility of reflecting 100 women's stories with integrity and accuracy and also battled the periodic isolation of sticking to my writing process. The other has helped me advance my own clarity about work I want to do up ahead. On top of these fairly concrete results, my moais have offered me a plethora of spiritual learning and reflection, as well as honest feedback about what my choices might mean.

Sandra Zimmer, age sixty-six, author and expert in public speaking and executive presence, is a member of one of these moais. About our moai meeting, she said, "It's amazing how often we come to the same or similar awareness in our own ways. What an affirmation. Coming together regularly I think we've transformed our work and personal lives by sharing and receiving loving support. The meetings are insightful and help keep me focused on what's important. Women in the group support me in ways I haven't had for many years. I especially value the spiritual wisdom we each bring to the calls."

Each of us in the moai of which Sandra spoke finds our regular connection a mainstay in our lives.

Never did my "sisters" tell me what to do or judge the conundrums I found myself in. My self-doubt was respected. So was my fatigue, my elation, my full-on drive. They skillfully mirror back to me what I'm saying each meeting, in their own words and with their own loving and insightful observations.

Because many of us who are fifty to seventy-plus have not been witnessed as much as men in our culture, it's powerful to experience spaces that welcome our emerging feminine insight, deep reflection, and birthing new ideas into form. Ideas that we articulate to wise listening ears have a far better chance of taking form in new behaviors and plans when incubated within the context of a supportive sisterhood.

However a moai comes about—naturally in the cultures into which we were born like the Blue Zones mentioned, or in ways we consciously create—we can identify the characteristics that set such impactful relationships apart from mere social engagements, however sweet the latter may be.

Moais are conscious. They're regular. They have a process or a ritual that is repeated, which is important for connection, trust, and focus.

It can be a lonely experience not having a moai or anything similar. Loneliness is something that elders in the developed world report in increasing numbers. Prime Minister Teresa May recognized loneliness and isolation as so serious in relation to people's well-being that she appointed a "minister of loneliness" in the UK.[16]

For many people, belonging to a religious community and having weekly or twice-weekly services, like my church offers, is a place for not only connection but for lifting up of our concept of ourselves. Spiritually, we are reminded of who we really are. But not everyone has such a religious community or has access to one. And not everyone wants one, especially people still healing from finding something other than an uplifting experience/theology where they once engaged with a religion.

I recall Brené Brown telling the story of her husband asking her what she really wanted as a result of her research. She thought quietly and then said, "That everyone in the world would feel comfortable speaking about vulnerability and shame. Because it's needed for healing." I realize, as I write this book, that I want every woman in the world to have a moai—a deep sisterhood made of the stuff I've described. There's no reason not to have

---

16 Jason Daly, "The U.K. Now Has a 'Minister of Loneliness': Here's Why It Matters" in Smithsonianmag.com (online), January 19, 2018. https://www.smithsonianmag.com/smart-news/minister-loneliness-appointed-united-kingdom-180967883/.

what is natural for our living and loving; for our need to feel connected and affirmed.

I'm personally committed to offering virtual moai groups after hearing the powerful impact they've had on the women I interviewed in addition to the power they've delivered in my life too. Sisterhoods like these are a gift we deserve to give ourselves in Adulthood II.

Create one. Join one. Redefine a group you're already in. Moais for women deserve to be a worldwide practice.

Story

Linda Pierce, seventy-one, has been retired since 1999. A demanding career arcing into very senior levels at a major oil and gas company, Linda's work required that she prove her value every day; in fact, prove she was more valuable Tuesday than she has been the previous Monday. "It was an environment of 'can't fail; one mistake and it's over,'" she said. Competitive would be a cultural understatement for the atmosphere within which Linda rose in the ranks and provided business transformation coaching and consultation to top level leaders.

Her retirement picture is what some may consider ideal: a traditional pension earned through many years of hard work, delivering ample choices about how to spend time now. Opportunities to travel. Hours for exercise and leisure, if desired. Though some of these activities are very much part of Linda's life, she is extremely conscious about her purpose and especially her continued growth.

"I'm big on self-organizing," she said. "I created a gyroscope to depict what comprises a full, diverse life with balance for myself. If you think of a pie, it has slices called Physical, Financial, Intellectual, Social, Joyful Well-Being, and Spiritual."

Over time, Linda found things shifting in the Social dimension. She realized something was missing. She invited two friends from her community to build a "sacred circle."

"They struck me as spiritual beings," Linda said, "open and perhaps willing to speak contrarian views about things that matter." The circle started meeting every two weeks with a revolving leadership. Each person rotates guiding the topic at each meeting. Starting with quiet meditation, they then have a short list of questions.

Each woman speaks in response to the questions, and the rest listen with no comment. When everyone has spoken, they reflect on the patterns: what was similar in their thinking and experiences, and what was different.

"The group has grown over the sixteen years we've been meeting," Linda shared by phone. "Three members have passed away, and others have joined. We hold an annual retreat now for our group. The women's circle helps deepen my authenticity and connect me to my soul which is sacred to me. There's nothing like the depth and meaningfulness of our listening and conversations. It's a very important part of my life."

QUOTES

"The world is calling for women to be who they authentically are. In a safe space we can all grow into what we're meant to be rather than from fear-based old ways."

—NIKKI T., FIFTY-SEVEN

"It's so meaningful to be in a group of women who are seeking to live purposefully. I feel a sense of belonging and mirroring that's immensely important. The openness in the group allows what's true for me to come forward. It's being understood and held."

—KATIE E., FIFTY-FIVE

"Ten years ago I felt very lonely. There was a missing part I really didn't know. To have found people I can even talk to—getting a network who speak the same language—I'm finally able to put the puzzle pieces together."

—INEZ S., LATE FIFTIES

Antidote To

This Declaration is an antidote to the expectation of loneliness or the notion it's impossible to form meaningful bonds of support in later years. An absence of lifelong friendships or easy situational conditions is not a self-fulfilling prophecy. New circles of deep connection can be created for these new times.

PRACTICE

Scan the women in your sphere of awareness. Do so with soft inner eyes, inviting a light expansive review rather than an analytical one. They may or may not be close by geographically—this exercise is just as valid for women who live at a distance, with whom you can connect by phone. They may be friends, associates, colleagues you've not seen for a while, neighbors, women at church or in your spiritual community, people you've met at lectures, classes, or workshops, those you hardly know but with whom you feel a connection. The soft scanning will bring into awareness women with whom you would enjoy engaging on topics that involve an interest in reflection and contemplation. They will naturally have the skill of listening, reciprocity of spirit, and reliability.

Don't be surprised if they aren't women in your usual social circles. Choose those with whom you feel a potential gentle bond.

Identify two you would feel comfortable reaching out to for an exploration of their interest in gathering regularly for lightly structured conversation on spiritual/contemplative/purpose-oriented topics. This is a distinctly different get-together than to discuss politics or share problems! Make this difference explicit.

The first step can be an invitation for an exploratory first gathering, with no pressure yet to commit. A good guideline for a first meeting is two hours max. Choose a quiet comfortable place such as one of your homes or quiet community space available to you. Use a simple outline for your own light facilitation at the first meeting. At the end, if you think the group makeup is conducive for follow-up meetings, ask whether participants would like to meet again. Schedule the meeting within three weeks if possible.

After you have met twice, codify the simple guidelines you've agreed to related to place, regularity, process, facilitation, and confidentiality.

DECLARATION 9

LEAVING YOUR LEGACY

*We are learning to pass along what
we have learned for the evolution
and perpetuity of good in the world.*

The challenge of Leaving Your Legacy may be poignant for many
of us who simply don't know how/when/with whom to do so.
But something core to who we are as humans yearns to capture
the best of ourselves, value it, and leave it for others. Our "others"
may not be younger people, per se. But across the board in the
100 interviews, there was a healthy search for how we might leave
things in a better state for future generations.

We also long for those in our sisterhood—that is, others our
age—to claim their voices and value the wisdom they've accrued,
not keeping it behind closed doors.

Leaving Your Legacy can sometimes feel like a luxury if the challenge of financial well-being is taking up a great deal of psychic energy. I was impressed to hear of the creative, resilient, and spunky ways women well over fifty are navigating issues of finances so they can follow their irrepressible legacy-leaving calls. Refusing to acquiesce to some of the weights that may loom about us is the beginning of finding our way through them.

Leaving Your Legacy is enacted in as many forms as the women considering how to do so. While Pioneering On is about continuing to self-express, Leaving Your Legacy has the flavor of consciously passing something along that will be accessible to others. These two may not be mutually exclusive, of course. But one—the latter—takes into account the consideration of time (not as much left) and the desire to imprint something specific in lasting form.

There were so many examples of how the women I interviewed were thinking on this topic. Like Debbie who went to Southern China at sixty-seven to enact what felt like "a diamond in her belly." Many of us feel these diamonds in our bellies—things we are compelled to enact and leave behind. They might come in the form of land to preserve or cohousing to create. A memoir to write. Grandkids and adult children to shower with undistracted presence, free of technology. These are a few of the many ways the 100 women I listened to expressed not only a desire but a *yearning* to leave the best of themselves for the benefit of others.

Joanna, sixty-four, spoke in our interview about legacy leaving as finding our sacred task; what we were put here to do. It's never too late to find and offer this gift.

For some women it may be codifying a lifetime of professional work for others to access. For others—especially those who have not spent time doing so until now—it may be taking time to identify and value the basic qualities of who we are "such as being a kind person, a good mother" as Joanna said, and identifying where we can apply this sacred task to make a lasting difference. "It's more than a vocation," she continued. "It's what the second half of life is about."

LEAVING A PROFESSIONAL IMPRINT

One form of Leaving Your Legacy relates to the work we've spent our careers developing, honing, perfecting. Along these lines, I heard two rhetorical questions from many of the women I interviewed:

Have I done everything I can yet?

How can I take what I've created in my life and pass it along for others to benefit?

Organizing, crystallizing, or packaging one's work so it benefits future generations can take many forms. Sandra Zimmer, sixty-four, wants to devote the years ahead to ensuring her public speaking program and system of overcoming stage fright will be available to people long after she's gone. While Sandra continues to teach her programs personally in Houston, Texas, she has also invested in a plan to record her teaching process on video with a workbook to coincide. Making *The Sandra Zimmer Method* a lasting offering after she's gone has been strong motivating energy for Sandra's effort.

Jo Lynam has a wholly different legacy plan at age fifty-nine. The mother of Emma who was born with Down syndrome and deafness, Jo and her husband were told to give up on their daughter.

Right in her hospital bed after a C-section delivery, Jo pronounced that Emma "would be known." She welcomed Emma with the expectation of her daughter living a purposeful life despite all the prognostications. Though she didn't necessarily expect to, Jo has dedicated her life to helping Emma become a happy and participating member of their community in Australia. Her tireless efforts, passionate advocacy, and breakthrough ideas every day of Emma's life have transcended predictions to such an inspiring degree that Jo and Emma were featured in an ABC television special.

Fast forward to the time of our interview: Jo had paved the way for Emma to be employed as an office paper shredder at a local company. By that time, Emma was living in her own flat and cooking for herself. She had the support of regular caseworkers in addition to Jo, went on her first vacation to Sea World and Dreamworld, and in 2017 took another one to Japan with a support worker who reported how honored she felt to have been part of this journey with Emma.

Moving beyond the tireless road of getting Emma to be independent, capable of living a safe and happy life long after her parents are gone, Jo knew she needed to pass along the hope and possibility of these results to other families. Her legacy is not only Emma but the business she is establishing, aimed at helping families with profoundly disabled children.

"We are all here for a reason," Jo said. "If you find your passion you find your path. Mine is to let families know that if Emma can defy all the odds, so can their children. We're all connected in helping each other. We as women are the ones to nurture our children's children. We can hear exactly what we're here for. Each of us can light a candle."

Said seventy-year-old Charlotte, "This is a time in life for harvesting my wisdom," and continuing her groundbreaking lifework in neuropsychology and spirituality as mentioned earlier. "I'm taking my defining moments and integrating them for a greater contribution. My own priority right now is to help people find out what they're here for."

"I don't think baby boomers have made their greatest contribution yet," Charlotte continued. "We have to sort out what we've learned and what we know. It's important to reflect on the wisdom we've gleaned and continue to create a sense of purpose from it for ourselves and others. It's empowering. It gives us meaning. It's a source of vitality. This is a time of integration and contribution."

I loved hearing the women I interviewed not only speak about specific ways they are endeavoring to Leave Your Legacy—large or small—but their *thinking* about the process.

Whereas we've been acculturated to think in terms of continued production—the usual definition of work—the idea behind Pioneering On and Leaving Your Legacy is connected to one's continued sense of becoming and valuing who we are. It's not about doing something just for others, come what may. It's about recognizing the wisdom and inner knowing we've gained over years of trials and challenges.

FOCUSING ON "THE GIVEAWAY"

Focusing on what we are here for now, saying no to things we are Done With, conserving energy for what's most purposeful, are all strategies for being able to Leave Your Legacy we want. "I thank God for what I've said no to," said Gigi, sixty-six. "I'm really connected to the need to say no so I can give attention to the 'yes' of what I'm to do, to offer, and perhaps to leave behind."

Gigi spoke of this being a time for listening: for the gifts she and others have for this time; for the stories we are here to carry, change, let go of, and give birth to. "I ask myself," she said, "how can we bring the gift of our voices to the world while making room for all voices—especially those heard least often?"

Betty Artes, sixty-two, shared her full story in chapter 4, "Anvil of Our Becoming." But beyond the tale of how she came into the restaurant business and came to find herself, is her legacy: The manifestation of a lifetime of influences—family, work, culture, personal experimentation—in the form of award-winning chili sauces and other Mexican-inspired recipes now bottled and distributed for the general public to enjoy.

Who says our gifts can't be made into legacies of all kinds—and flavors?

I learned the indigenous concept of a "giveaway" during the 100-women interview process as it relates to Leaving Your Legacy. "The giveaway" is finding a medium, a passage, or an environment where one's gifts can be shared; where fulfillment comes to us by sharing our wisdom with others. It's not about "doing" per se—not efforting—but "pursuit of a certain way of being" in Pam's words. It's listening for situations and places where our sacred uniqueness can be enacted. Pam's "giveaway" came in the form of being asked to serve on the board of the School of Lost Borders. "When the invitation came, I felt like I was being seen for who I am and what I know," she said at seventy-four. "There's a wonderful reward in it, but reward is not the goal."

Women well over fifty need to be seen. Our wisdom is needed. It's useful. It's practical. It's immensely wise because it's backed by hard-earned lessons from trials, losses, triumphs, stark and shocking experiences with a range of conditions and realities of the human spirit. It comes from maneuvering and, for some, mothering in a system that was not designed to accommodate intuition and receptive awareness alongside diligence and agency.

At a time when the prevailing culture has traditionally dismissed women in our mid-fifties and beyond, women are stepping up to model what Pioneering On, Leaving Your Legacy, and mentoring younger women can do for transformational change in the world.

As Deborah, fifty-eight, said, "Our culture is craving community and openness, the wisdom from the past for application to the present. We don't know we're craving it, but the signs are everywhere."

Christina is doing just that at seventy as she leaves her legacy. Mentioned earlier as founder of the practice and author of the book *The Circle Way*, in addition to several other books, she said in our interview, "I see women saying, 'I have one more shot,' and asking what the remaining thing is that they must do. Since I myself would be happy to never step on an airplane again after all my years of teaching and leading workshops, we decided we had to hand off the Circle Way work to others. It took three years to decide how to do it. But we threw the ball and the next generation caught it…and we have practitioners in the thousands now."

LEAVING AN IMPRINT AS MENTORS

Organizing one's body of knowledge for the sake of perpetuity has a link to another major theme of legacy leaving. Mentoring others, especially younger women and grandchildren, came through not just as a desirable duty but as an irrepressible desire. Sage Dawna, seventy-five, said of this urge, "It's in the natural order to pass things along from one to another."

Where loving and mentoring grandchildren has ingredients of undistracted presence, tremendous love and attention, and being available in small ways for their exquisite moments of becoming, mentoring younger women has ingredients of conscious time set aside to pass along particular skills, lessons, and counsel. In other words, grandparenting has an informal rhythm to it, where mentoring often has more structure, intention, and planning built in.

Wendy, Carole, Dawna, and Lois already feel catalyzed to develop and provide supportive counsel to younger women.

Wendy, fifty-seven, is part of a network called The Coaching Fellowship providing pro bono coaching to young women social impact entrepreneurs. She finds this work more satisfying than anything else as she juggles it with continued sales of her best-selling book and co-founding her new company with two women partners.

Carol Wilburn, sixty-one, calls herself a "communitarian" as well as permaculture designer and teacher for restorative urban lifestyles. She is living her belief that women already have gifts and are already doing things that are incredible in the world. She sees it as an important task for women to claim what they can pass along, as she herself is doing.

"I don't have a house or car anymore," said Carol. "I've let my life become much simpler. It's about being of service now to people close to me and in larger ways too. I'm starting a cross-generational land-based community called Phoenixes Rising through which I'll be supporting and teaching young people to live a different, simpler way. Whenever I feel sad or discouraged, it's easy for me to feel 'done.' But it inspires me hearing stories of other human beings who are daring to live differently; who have the courage to ask or follow through on something different that's calling. I can know that I'm not crazy; I'm not alone; there are others on this path."

Dawna, seventy-five, called herself a "legacy bearer." She consciously opens space for nine women who can apply to be mentored. I loved the generosity of this idea and the practicality of having the relationship defined with this kind of intentional commitment. "I'm compelled to work with women," Dawna said, "and find it a natural order to pass wisdom on from one to the next generation." She considers herself a thinking partner rather than a coach, helping women create stability on the inside for increasingly unstable times on the outside.

"We must risk our significance," she shared with me in our interview, "and find what really matters. Our attention is powerful, and what has been discovered recently in neuroscience is that where attention goes, neurons grow. We can choose what to give our attention to. Where power is a man's currency, *influence* can be woman's currency," she continued. "This is part of what I want to share with others." Not surprisingly, Dawna's new book is titled *Living a Loved Life: Awakening Wisdom through Stories of Inspiration, Challenge, and Possibility*.

Lois Shannon, fifty-four, literally rearranged her life and that of her family's to mentor younger women and contribute to a growing movement that lauds and supports women in leadership. A background working at Apple and named in *The Wall Street Journal* on a short list of high-powered women in 1999, Lois made a choice for full-time motherhood after giving birth to three children in four years.

Her move to France and focus on motherhood in her children's earlier years led to tremendous self-discoveries about healthy mothering and what she considered a calling to address issues of mothering and womanhood from a deeper place. Recognizing an awakening happening with women at this time to support and nurture each other and for each to become who she truly is, Lois came across a then newly forming organization founded by Chantal Pierrat called Emerging Women. Lois realized she needed to geographically move again in order to support Chantal's effort in a boots-on-the-ground way. "I thrive on my connection to women," she said. "It's my purpose and it feeds me."

"I think we're going toward a massive awakening," Lois continued. "Women are especially waking up to who we are. So many women in our fifties and sixties have huge potential to be leaders in this movement and this awakening! We can support each other in it. It's scary if we think we're doing it alone. We're carrying a lot of patriarchy. But we can help each other. We can share our stories. This is a time when we have so much fear, but I am hopeful. I feel joy. I think we're in for a rough road…" she added, "but women are going to lead this."

As I write this, I relate to the women who may not find obvious ways to mentor yet. Both writing this book to pass along the collective wisdom of women over fifty, and spending time with my loved eleven-year-old youngster-friend Batia, is how I am consciously passing along what I've learned. I had the delight of Batia formally asking me in writing if I would be one of her mentors as she enters adolescence. How fun and touching to say yes to this! And needless to say, her over-fifty mother had the wisdom to facilitate her daughter's seeking of counsel from those of us who have insights about what's ahead. I'm not sure it all feels substantial enough (yet) in terms of a legacy…but I am reflecting on the wisdom I've gained from these interviews and willing to hear what other diamonds are in my belly to pass along or imprint in some way.

Meg Wolitzer, author of the new novel *The Female Persuasion*, was reflecting on the mentors in her life in her interview with *Marie Claire* magazine.[17] She said, "I don't think I ever thought, you are my mentor. When someone sees something in you, you start wanting to please them. The way you feel when you're seen, maybe for the first time—it makes you want to be better, to take yourself seriously."

I love that! What a grand way for us to mentor others informally! To see other women; to compliment what we see them doing well, making them want to step into pleasing us and the high calling we see in them. The ripple effect is more substantial than we think.

I keep in mind sixty-four-year-old Wales interviewee Pippa Bondy's statement; a woman who created a foundation to bring ancient healing arts and modern methods together and does a lot of mentoring through outdoor wilderness guiding and teaching of the Alexander Technique. She said she absolutely loves her role as a mentor. "I'm not a Gandhi or an Obama. But I have my piece to do for a good effect on our planet."

The size of what we've done so far in life doesn't matter. As outlined in chapter 4, "Anvil of Our Becoming": it's not about the doing we've done, it's about the *being* we manifest.

MENTORING WHERE THERE'S NO "VILLAGE"
Christina B. raised a rhetorical question for those of us at this

---

17 "The Second Sex" in Storytellers section, *Marie Claire* magazine, April 2018, 111.

stage of life, including herself at seventy, who want to be engaged in passing along our knowledge and wisdom: How can you be an elder in the absence of a village?

Indeed, traditional eldering with its elements of mentoring and skill sharing have historically been carried out in a town or a village. This is certainly true in the Blue Zones mentioned in chapter 8, "Create a Moai." But that traditional paradigm paralyzes the mentoring we can do in new modern configurations of life.

Wendy, Dawna, Lois, and many other women are redefining "village" to include youngers who live anywhere in the world. And why not, since technology allows this kind of meaningful mentoring?

Mentoring may be in our apartment complexes or immediate neighborhoods. One women talked about her father who, in his later years "adopted all the neighborhood children." As we think in creative ways and listen for opportunities to become involved with others who need our skills or presence, those opportunities can come. We can create what I call "village moments" wherever we are.

GRANDPARENTING

Another wholly unique form of mentoring—though far more than that—is the role of grandparenting as part of legacy leaving.

Not only is being a grandparent a way women fifty to seventy-plus feel they are playing a helpful role in the becoming of another person, but the joy and deeply fulfilling space it occupies was one that many interviewees found hard to describe. In fact, it wasn't spoken of as a legacy-leaving goal, per se, though I heard threads of that in women's comments.

I came across a statement in a *New York Times* op-ed by a man named Jim Sollisch who listed his bio thus: "Mr. Sollisch is a grandfather."[18] His piece was about just that. The teaser subtitle for the article was the same sentiment I heard in so many of the 100 interviews related to grandparenting. "I have raised five children. But I have never felt this pure, unfettered happiness."

Grandparenting becomes a significant role for some women, bringing with it new depths of love and awe about life itself. This depends on one's relationship with her adult children as well as geographic proximity and the amount of time she wants to spend as a backup caretaker and/or involved adult in grandchildren's lives, of course.

One woman told me of her own mother's comment when she had children. "Don't expect me to come and help with your kids!" her mother had said. "I'm done!" This motivated Kara, sixty-three, to be the opposite with her children's children, loving her involvement in her grandchildren's lives.

A few of the women I interviewed have structured their lives to make themselves available nearly 100 percent to their grandchildren—which other women see as a pitfall. Still others choose to be lovingly involved as regularly and geographically feasible as possible while still pursuing other lines of personal development and outward service.

Levels of involvement, and both the desire and invitation to actively grandparent, is different from one woman to another. But an outstanding theme within it is the special quality of love that is experienced toward one's children's children. "No one can

18   Jim Sollisch, "The Particular Joy of Being a Grandparent," *The New York Times* Opinion section, 3 August, 2018. A19.

replace me when it comes to family," said Cindy W., sixty, as she reflected on the legacy she is planning to leave related to her considerable life work. "That's where I want to spend a lot of my time now."

Fiona, sixty-three, talked about how much she was impacted by the work of Tim McCarthy[19] when considering the legacy she wants to leave. "Every action I take—every decision—should do no harm to children seven generations from now. For me this includes the rocks, trees, plants, animals. And of course my eight grandchildren who are so very important in my life. They have triggered so much internal change in me and the expression of so much love and appreciation for this beautiful world we live in. I have an increased appreciation for humanity with all its foibles and faults, heroism, ingenuity, courage, and love. I love watching these little beings form the person they will carry into the world."

Fiona expressed the distinct quality of tenderness and unconditional love I heard in the voices of many women who spoke of grandchildren as a priority in their lives and part of the legacy to which they want to contribute. To my ears, it is quite different than mentoring.

Where mentoring is passing specific information, counsel, and yes, love, along, grandparenting had a distinct flavor of being softened with love in a way that nothing else does. I don't have this experience yet in my own life in terms of grandchildren, though I have the blessing of a beloved eleven-year-old who fills my heart with sparkling joy unlike any other relationship.

---

19   Tim McCarthy, "Rethink Progress," TEDx Trinity College l TED, 18 April 2015.

Grandparenting is just as much in the *receiving* of life and love as in the giving.

Obviously this need not only be the terrain of biological connections. Scotty Sanders, now seventy-eight, has rearranged her entire life to live close to the children she wants to mentor and grandparent. "Show them the mistakes you've made!" she declared. "Give them advice, help them decide what's important at this time in their lives."

Ann Linnea, sixty-seven, is a writer and educator who "embodies the stewardship of wild things" as an outdoor guide, environmentalist, and true pioneer of the sea (read: first woman to circumnavigate Lake Superior by sea kayak). She blends her lifelong study of nature with both mentoring and grandparenting.

"I want my grandchildren to feel hopeful," she said. "I want them to realize their greatest potential. I wish every child in the world could feel the ability to reach his/her fullest abilities." She continues. "It's a great gift to be outdoors with children doing anything—just being. Digging sandcastles. Experiencing the patterns in nature. We feel more spacious when outdoors. This is something we can pass along to youngers. It connects us to something larger than ourselves. I encourage it of parents and of grandparents."

Many a woman whose children have had children finds this new territory far more meaningful than they imagined.

It may or may not include long periods of time or the crossing of daily lives. But this domain of love and the priority it takes for many people in Adulthood II is an informal part of the legacy they are leaving and want to leave—the opportunity to witness and support a young person's process of becoming and to be a source of unconditional love that benefits both.

"If I ache at all," said Maggie Weiss, sixty-two, "it's because we just don't see what a miracle we are. Humans are the biggest force on the planet. The fact that we understand each other as much as we do—that we ourselves are such a miracle—if there's anything I want to leave my son and others, it's that."

THE WEIGHTS THAT LEAD TO LEGACIES

For some of us, yearning to Leave Your Legacy is a natural outgrowth of wanting to address things that weigh heavily on us. We become more aware of the state of things being left to our youngers as the big picture becomes more apparent—and perhaps because our love takes on a different quality, too.

For my interview question, *"What weighs on you the most at this time in your life?"* I heard definite themes in the 100 responses. These pain points can be lighthouses for those who may be seeking ways to contribute for future generations. Sages and philosophers, including British author and religious scholar and teacher Andrew Harvey, recommend that a good place to start for finding one's purpose—especially if natural attraction to something isn't lighting you up—is to identify what's breaking your heart. It may hint at where we want to add our grains of sand to the sandbags of fortification against rising tides of the world's problems.

WEIGHT ONE: THE BIG GLOBAL CONUNDRUM

The number one response to what weighs on the 100 women I interviewed is under the headline "the big global conundrum." Global warming, health of the planet, partisan politics, lack of respectful discourse, a dismantling of democracy and shared democratic principles worldwide, rising inhumanity toward immigrants and others, loss of civility, and animal abuse were among the topics.

The majority of the 100 women I interviewed took long, quiet pauses when identifying these overwhelmingly complex—and saddening—issues. I could hear the awareness and concern of how vast these weights felt to each woman voicing them, punctuated by sighs and silence. Interestingly though, none of them descended into the depths of despair, but rather collected themselves in some manner with a statement of "but we can all play our part…" or "but I have vowed to do my piece of what can be done." The polarity of deep concern and personal resolve was marked.

WEIGHT TWO: EXISTENTIAL ISSUES

This category of weights I call existential in nature. The isolation and loneliness that go hand-in-hand with no longer being part of a workforce. Some sadness in experiencing what one woman perceives as "the last one"—e.g.: the last car I might buy; the last sofa I might ever pick out. Regrets about having hurt people in the past. Wishing more time had been spent with one's children while they were growing up.

WEIGHT THREE: INSIDER KNOWLEDGE

Some topics women identified as weights were derived from close-up familiarity with particular lines of work. The rise of autism in children was one. Overuse of pharmaceuticals was another. Increasing reliance on cell phones and email for communication, as well as the addiction they incite, thereby decreasing intimate bonds between parents and their young children. The use of social media was mentioned many times by many women. And of course, the noticeable change in tree life, forest undergrowth, and water was another, with examples from the nearby ecosystems where several interviewees live, study, and write in the US, Europe, and in Australia.

These issues that weigh on women have become in some cases catalysts for Leaving Your Legacy in order to help bend the arc of future behavior toward better, healthier outcomes.

WEIGHT FOUR: PERSONAL FINANCES

While some of the 100 women have accrued manageable if not abundant retirement benefits through pension plans, stock options, and the opportunity to invest discretionary funds over a long period of time, such is not the case with many. The weight of limited finances, whether real or perceived, is one that can occupy much thought and energy for women mid-fifties and beyond, potentially draining us from being able to focus on the long-term legacy we would otherwise want to leave.

I found this concern mostly showing up with women who chose nontraditional careers and/or worked in not-for-profits, changed jobs, took time out to raise children, worked part time, or were self-employed. All of these interviewees shared very real questions about whether their finances will last long enough to support a long lifespan. Some reflected on the reality that they would have planned better had they done it again. Many said it's an important message they want to give younger women: plan ahead, don't be dumb, keep the strategic picture of your life in mind as you manage your finances.

Roshana Ariel, sixty-one, knows exactly what her retirement funds are. She received them at age sixty after twenty-five years in the newspaper business, including a role as managing editor. She chose a new path after living long enough with the stress, noise, and distraction of the newsroom experience. Deciding to end her employment for a company, she began researching intentional communities around the US where she might live on basic funds. She weighed options, including geographic location, cost effectiveness, and details about the community, that would best suit her priorities. She initially chose a cohousing community where she lived in a straw bale house in exchange for working various jobs in the community. It wasn't for her.

"I thought, 'What am I doing?'" she recalled. "It's hot and all my stuff is covered in dirt!" She gave herself the gift of a retreat that provided structure and support to reflect on her next steps. "My depression lifted," Roshana said. She researched another community in Colorado and made a commitment to move there. "It's harder than I thought in some ways," she said, "but I'm slowly settling in. People worry that they're the only ones worried about certain things. It helps to have other women's feedback, perspective, and wisdom. We're really not alone in these things that we're trying to figure out."

In fact, many women I interviewed made choices about where, and how, to live based upon their finances and their desires to live within their means in order to answer a legacy-leaving call, whether small or large.

For instance, Elizabeth, fifty-eight, took over her family's cabin in a rural lake district of northern Minnesota, a dirt road winding through the trees for nearly a mile before reaching the small, wood structure. This was not reflective of a scenario she would have imagined herself choosing. "My friends cannot understand why

I'm here," she said. "And sometimes I'm surprised I'm here too! But I trust that one step will lead to another. In my life, every single thing that has happened has been for a purpose and has helped the next one. This will be one also."

Norma, sixty-five, rents a room in a stately mansion at the feet of her town's mountains. "I have a system of keeping seasonal things in a small storage unit," she said. "I rotate them each season and redecorate my space regularly. It's much easier to travel light."

Sunny, sixty-three, envisioned a way to split her home into two completely private sections and rents out the bottom portion, allowing her to stay in the neighborhood she loves.

Downsizing, cohousing, living in a transit van, renting out rooms in one's home, having several rooms in different parts of the country between which to travel—these are all creative choices women well over fifty have made at least partly due to financial considerations. Such nontraditional ways of living, not seen in retirement eras of the past, can free women from the heaviness of regular mortgages or homecare responsibilities and liberate their energies to create new paths or work on what's important to them.

That's not to say it's easy. Many an interviewee said finances cause worry at times, especially if health or mobility issues become a priority. But nearly every interviewee who said this also said she trusts that, as she continues to think through options and make choices wisely, it will work out somehow.

"My relationship to value is changing," said Liz Gunn at fifty-four. "I have faith in the unknown-ness of the future. I'm not tied to a traditional look at worth or money. I was really tested on this. But my relationship to what is enough has changed."

WEIGHT FIVE: FUTURE CARE NEEDS

Related to finances, the women I interviewed referenced questions that come up in the back of their minds about potential care-taking needs they might have if their mobility or independence were interrupted. These questions were heightened if there were no adult children or if one's adult children weren't available or weren't prone to support in this way.

The concern about long-term care fell into two categories across the women I interviewed:

- I don't have anyone in my circle/family who is poised to help care for me if there's a need.
- I don't want to be a burden on my children and want to figure out a way to have my needs met if something comes up.

For women who fall into the above two categories, and absent the availability, privilege, and comfort of a solid healthcare plan backed by secure health insurance, potential healthcare needs remain an active question; one that many women are mindful of and determined not to be overwhelmed by. Nevertheless, it's a weight some of us carry while Pioneering On and Leaving Our Legacy.

For women in our fifties, sixties, seventies, eighties, it's crucially important to share our stories and challenges, especially about the truly unique ways we are laying down new tracks for what these years can look like if without handsome pension plans. It's also important to share some of the ways we are meeting and dealing with them successfully. Our collective stories are important as lights on the path for others.

I recall at the end of one interview, a woman in her seventies who was full of wisdom paused after sharing what she hoped would come from a book like this. Thinking quietly about women over fifty she said, "You know, just managing ourselves is doing much."

I cannot count how many times that sentence has spoken to me when I've been navigating my own way forward. Some days it feels like one step forward and three back. Like the phrase my friend Jeff Salzman uses: sometimes we fail forward. That's what it feels like as we cut through the thicket of various wilderness periods, especially as pioneers in the age of active wisdom.

But take heart. Just managing ourselves is doing much.

A Valley Like This

Sometimes you look at an empty valley like this,
and suddenly the air is filled with snow.
That is the way the whole world happened—
there was nothing, and then...
But maybe some time you will look and even
the mountains are gone, the world becomes nothing
again. What can a person do to help
bring back the world?
We have to watch and then look at each other.
Together we hold it close and carefully
save it, like a bubble that can disappear
if we don't watch out.
Please think about this as you go on. Breathe on the world.
Hold out your hands to it. When the mornings and evenings
roll along, watch how they open and close, how they
invite you to the long party that your life is.

—WILLIAM STAFFORD[20]

20 William Stafford, "A Valley Like This," in *Even Quiet Places* (Minneapolis, MN: Graywolf Press, 2010).

NEW ROLES AS PIONEERS

I contend that a big part of our legacy right now as women over fifty—especially women in their sixties and seventies—is raising new questions and supporting each other as we experiment during this new phase. Whatever is ours to do and leave, we can be encouraged again by the words of Linda in her seventies: "Like Olympians, we run *through* the line, not to it." I sensed throughout the 100 interviews how much we need that reminder. The presence of our wisdom, resilience, compassion, and activism is desperately needed in a world announcing its readiness every day for the truths in *A Call to Further Becoming*, carried in the bones of 100, 1,000, 1,000,000 women over age fifty.

As the preachers say: May it be so.

Or rather: May we *make* it so.

● *Story* ●

Jerilyn DeCoteau, sixty-seven, grew up on a reservation in North Dakota during part of her childhood years. A proud member of the Turtle Mountain Band of the Chippewa, she graduated valedictorian from its high school and applied immediately for college though pregnant with her and her husband's first child. While devoted to her baby daughter's early years, Jerilyn managed to earn a BA in English and go on for her master's in education. Already motivated to help her Native people, Jerilyn went back to the reservation to work at the newly founded tribal college. Eventually serving on the local school board and becoming involved with tribal issues, observers of Jerilyn's leadership skills, passion, and intellect led to their suggestion that she pursue law school. In a pre-law summer session for Native students, Jerilyn took her LSAT and was immediately admitted into law school.

By then, Jerilyn was the mother of two. Undaunted by the demands of law school plus parenting, she continued the ardent path toward a law degree, a divorce during the time notwithstanding. Now a single mother with two daughters twelve and five, Jerilyn managed a difficult feat: doing well in law school and passing the bar while actively parenting her girls.

Marrying a second time to a man she met while studying law, Jerilyn moved to Colorado in order to work for the Native American Rights Fund. Her mission to "make Native communities stronger and more independent" led to working for the Indian Resources Section in the Department of Justice in Denver. With her youngest son still in high school, Jerilyn wanted to work in a position where regular travel was not required. She accepted a position running the Indian Clinic at University of Colorado Law School, and later taught Indian law at the University of Denver

Law School. In her late fifties, Jerilyn became involved with the First Nations Development Institute, leading their Asset Building Initiative and focusing on capacity building with tribes.

At sixty-one, Jerilyn was diagnosed with breast cancer. Surgery, chemotherapy and radiation, and the demand of radical self-care led to a decision to pursue part-time rather than full-time work. Even with an impressive resume, groundbreaking work with Native rights, a law degree and hard-earned life experience delivering not only knowledge but tremendous wisdom and chutzpah, at her age Jerilyn did not easily find part-time work in her field.

"I got my kicks in the teeth later in life," she said, referring to the difficulty courageous reformers like herself can face when working within any structure or in finding an outlet for their considerable education and lived experience—a sentiment to which many of the 100 women I interviewed relate.

Now president of the Board for the National Native American Boarding School Healing Coalition, Jerilyn can easily identify the legacy she wants to leave, whatever it takes. "I'm taking my background as an Indian attorney, and my experience living and working on a reservation, and using it now as a judge for a small tribe in New Mexico," she said. On the Supreme Court of the Pueblo de San Ildefonso, she's dedicated to helping them make a transition to a new form of government, one with a separation of powers and toward greater strength and independence.

"It's daunting—thrilling—seeing these people take risks," Jerilyn said. "They are making a sea-change in the way they govern, and it is awesome. I feel the weight of their trust. I have to do this—to be connected to Native communities. It's soul feeding and also very scary. And it's absolutely one of the deepest experiences of my life."

QUOTES

"For women, this is a time to look at the legacy of your life. What have I done?—not in a huge, grand way, but in the conversations you have within yourself. How do I complete what I'm doing here? How am I going to hold integrity in my life? We all need a story line to keep it together. Women may not identify themselves as pioneers, but they really are. We can all get on the train that says 'I claim my empowerment; my voice. That alone is important work to do.'"

—CHRISTINA B., SEVENTY

"I was raised by an African American mother from the Maasai tribe and a father with Lakota and Irish heritage. My grandfather was a bishop in the Colored Methodist Episcopal Church in the South, so I combined his influence with my father's sense of Native American spirituality. Navigating being Black in a white world, and looking white in a Black world due to my light skin, I lived between many worlds. As a result, I try to integrate my spiritual, racial, and social justice paths to help my college students know that their experiences are much more than just the life they seem to be born into. I realize my job is to show up as my authentic self with what I have to give—for my students, my five granddaughters, my friends. It's a legacy I want to leave, but it's even more than that: I try to establish safety and rapport for whatever deep conversations we can have. My desire is to help expand their perspectives to the extent they want it. Everyone has the authority to be a leader. Everyone can express leadership presence and influence the good in others. My aim is about being my authentic self for every teachable moment that shows up."

—MASAI J., SIXTY-NINE

"Any of us who have successfully achieved something want to share it and help others. This is a time to go back to one's basic personality I think. Get to the essence of who you really are—not your jobs, but the components of yourself—the essence of who you are. Through all *the life experiences and lessons learned, find where to give back. Find a need in the world and plug in. If everyone gives back, the world would be an even more wonderful place."*

—RETIRED COLONEL LYNN H., SIXTY-NINE

❧ *Antidote To* ❧

This Declaration is an antidote to the absence of a village where our wisdom might otherwise have been captured. There may not be a traditional village, per se, to receive our lifework and lessons. But we can create 'village moments' with those we seek out, or those who come into our lives. Or we can pass along our works (written, painted, sung, built, recorded, spoken, gifted) for those in the future whom we may not personally meet.

PRACTICE

Leaving Your Legacy means leaving an imprint that remains after we are physically gone. Whether we're aware of it or not, we all leave an imprint from the sheer act of being here and being a unique individual who lived and loved the way we did! After someone is gone, how many times do we hear, "She had no idea how much her words meant to me." "She was there right when I needed her." "I loved when we would just walk by the lake; bake cookies; sit quietly and read in the same room; go to plays."

Leaving Your Legacy may involve tangible actions in concrete forms. Or it may involve relational actions such as spending more time with those we love. We can choose where, how, and with whom we want to deepen our imprint.

Think of a "Celebration of Life" service held in your honor many years down the road. Imagine the groups of people represented there—different for each woman reading this. Examples are friends, family members, colleagues and ex-colleagues, neighbors, members of groups to which you belonged, church associates, former or current clients, students, patients, business partners.

Imagine your group to also include people who don't know your name but whom you came into contact where you volunteered or regularly shopped.

Write at least half a page on what you would WANT them to say about you at your remembrance celebration. (Note: this is different than imagining what they *would* say.) Let the words flow onto the page that reflect your fondest hopes and deepest desires for the lasting fragrance left by the irreplaceable you.

Then, let this be your legacy guide.

DECLARATION 10

EXQUISITE BEING

We are learning to relish the
magic of the ordinary.

I wrestled with the nub of this final theme. In fact, it sent me back to review all 700 pages of interview notes for a fourth time. The essence of this point felt so important and at first, harder to identify. It unmistakably had to do with being as opposed to doing; that I knew. It wasn't passive. It wasn't ethereal either. Then I happened upon Carol M.'s phrase once again and realized it was exactly what the 100 women were saying: Relish. Ordinary. Magic.

Repeatedly, my interviewees from fifty to ninety-three reflected on how life's riches are found for us in the preciousness of moments.

Whereas the principle Inhabit Beauty has a relationship to the rich suite of beauty's expression in art, music, colors, nature, the moments we find as Ordinary Magic include those things and more, particularly related to connecting with other living beings. Love is at the core. Relationships of appreciation and "grateful noticing" toward things small and large: family, strangers, wild animals, snow, friendly barking dogs like Piper and Dixie who live next to me, one's neighborhood, passersby, radiant baristas serving up our lattes. Nature in all its manifestations. Cups of tea; light. The way the leaves look against a brilliant blue sky.

These things may sound simplistic or overused, but I heard them spoken with voices of humble awe, perhaps because they were interlaced with women tracing their stories of loss, lessons, and love.

When I asked the 100 women about nonnegotiable practices, some women talked about striving to embody a meditative or prayerful state of thought throughout the day. Around this theme, women often referred to "living from the heart"; "living in the moment." I discern this to mean what I call living from the Higher Self. For women endeavoring to practice it, even in small degrees, it seems to give joy to everything. Noticing is the action. Gratefulness is the currency. Awe and wonder are the effects. They seem to feed on themselves and expand.

"The way I *am* is my work now," said Virginia, sixty-one.

"I believe we are made in the fabric of love," said Dodi Jackson, seventy, a longtime special education teacher, artist, and woman who considers her spiritual life and practices to be the guiding force of her life. "There are ways each of us can find that we can be love. It keeps us enchanted with life."

"As best I can, I hold the living of my life as ceremony," said sixty-six-year-old Gigi. "When I walk, when I meditate—in whatever administrative or fundraising or leadership work I'm engaged in."

Other phrases I heard about "Exquisite Being":

- The notion of being an instrument for a larger energy.
- Listening moment to moment about what we are called to do.
- Trying to be bright.
- Living life with as much truth as possible.

BEING PRESENT TO MOMENTS WITH OTHERS

Being available to our spouses/partners and to our grandchildren and children is another way we experience this kind of radiant awareness in given moments.

"We've been together three years now and are working on having the best relationship possible as two very conscious and developing people," said an interviewee at sixty who asked to remain anonymous. "I am exceedingly happy and amazed at some of the moments we have where we are helping one another grow."

"Being in a new marriage—a new relationship—has taken a lot of my focus this past year," said another woman at seventy-one. "Attending to the relationship has put other things on the back burner, especially as we combine households."

In cases when spousal relationships were mentioned, it was clearly a two-way gift for these women, carving out purposeful opportunities for deeper and more meaningful connection with one another.

Grandparenting was discussed at length in chapter 9, "Leaving Your Legacy" and clearly represents a domain that brings sparkling moments of mutual magic. The spontaneity that happens when traveling through life with a child who is actively learning and expressing is a unique type of exquisiteness.

So, too, is the kind of attention we give to our adult children.

Several days before writing this chapter, I took my son to see *Les Misérables* in Denver. Having purchased the tickets months earlier, we arrived to find they had given me confirmation for the right time but the wrong day. I had long cherished having Sam experience this musical since my daughter and I had seen it in London and talked about it ever since.

The whole outing in Denver seemed in jeopardy as we stood at the "Will Call" window trying to sort it out. My proof of purchase as offering of the expensive seats we'd paid for, I asked what seats were still available, imagining the 'day of' performance for the most popular musical in the world to be…slim. I turned to my son and said, "It's so right for us to see this today! We are going to see it." Just then the ticket host looked at his computer and said, "Wow—two tickets were just returned for good seats on the floor. I can give them to you at 50 percent off." Done!

We took our row M seats on the main floor, a fabulous view of the stage and far superior to the nosebleed section seats I'd prearranged. I was in grateful awe. When the performance opened with its grand musical burst Da Da DA…my whole being drank in the scene. Little did my son know that while he was growing up, a phrase from one of the songs was part of my prayer whenever he or my daughter were having challenges. When the character Jean Valjean sang, "And I will raise him to the light…" tears streamed down my face. I knew Sam would just think I was a sappy theatre goer (I am) rather than a mom who would hold that moment as absolutely exquisite; one I will never forget.

Such moments we, as women, do not take for granted. Ordinary magic, indeed.

Deborah, age fifty-eight, told me she loved motherhood more than all else she did in her decades-long still-continuing career. "My mother emphasized being open, curious, and childlike," she said. "When we're present with someone, we're there for what they offer and what we can learn. Being present, growing, and preserving those childlike qualities and passion is what's most important to me now."

"After all my years of keeping an intense schedule, I'm fully OK with just being," said Rhonda, sixty-one, who retired from her role as general manager at one of the world's largest energy companies. "Relationships are what's important."

Cindy W. reflected something similar. "I try to show up as love every day and the roles will figure themselves out."

RADIANT MOMENTS WITH EVERYONE AND ANYONE

Sometimes the "others" to whom we show up are not family or even friends. The magic of the ordinary can happen when we travel locally as well as in more exotic ways.

Though Zoe, seventy-three, makes a point of keeping in touch with friends, she embodies a spirit of other orientation toward every person who walks through the door at Pike Market Senior Center housed downstairs at the famous Pike Place Market. The market is bustling every day, familiar to any of us who have visited Seattle. Relationships with the market vendors are important from a personal and a donation standpoint, helping make a link between the community and seniors who qualify for the food and housing assistance to which Zoe is connected.

"Any service I do is prayer," said Zoe. If such is the case, Zoe is known for her daily, untiring, relationship-centered "prayer" for a huge swath of Seattle's people.

I love what Dawna reminded us earlier. "How powerful our attention is! We can choose where to give it."

Sunny, a volunteer since age sixty-two for a food bank on the opposite coast from Zoe, described this moment.

A young man had come in for food on a shift specifically for residents with no kitchens, e.g.: people who are homeless. He was skinny, tattooed from neck to fingertips including his shirtless chest and stomach, with matted dreadlocks; muttering. She took him through the food line. "He was talking to the cereal boxes, something about angels and pretzels," she said. "I called him by his name, Thomas, and he immediately responded like he was coming back to himself."

That day an unusual donation had come in of fresh potato salad in individual containers. She offered him some. He lit up. Back in the waiting area after he'd selected that day's food, she walked out to retrieve another shopping client and there sat Thomas, potato salad container popped open, quietly eating and appearing to savor it.

"I glanced at him and thought, 'He is the epitome of a misfit.' Everything we typically reject—dirty, disheveled, socially disconnected, tattooed, smelly, and seemingly in another world. The picture of an outcast. But at that moment, I saw his gratitude, enjoying that potato salad."

"He was so quiet," she said. "I saw how precious he was, and I was just washed with love for him. I said, 'How is it, Thomas?' He smiled, his eyes gleaming not with the delusions he sometimes gets, but with real connection. 'Oh, so good,' he said.

"For me," she concluded, "the moment was just beautiful."

Noticing is the posture of this theme. Gratitude plays a central role too.

No funds are required. No tickets are needed ahead of time. There are no preferred customers and no wait.

Seeing the magic of ordinary moments enlarges the presence of exquisiteness.

BEING PRESENT TO GOODNESS AND LOVE

"What's most important," said Barbara, "is the alive awareness I have that Source is animating my life. I'm full of energy and passion. I feel as if I'm being lived by Love—more creative energy than ever before. The two words I would use are alive and awake…and this at sixty-six!"

Liz, fifty-four, expressed something similar. "I make it a point to be attentive. I'm always in conversation with Spirit, Source. I'm amazed that I am the person I always wanted to be after doing all the work. I look in the mirror…and see I'm solidly in myself in a calm, self-assured, nonjudgmental way. I'm extremely grateful for this. I spend time every single morning looking at what's showing up that needs attention."

There seems to be a link between being open and childlike and noticing our own awe and animation. I loved hearing women express this in fresh ways!

"I was never more astonished to discover that the person I was at six years old is who I am now. It's worth taking a look at the child within us and cherishing it," said Karen from Australia at sixty-one.

Messenger

My work is loving the world.
Here the sunflowers, there the hummingbird—
equal seekers of sweetness.
Here the quickening yeast; there the blue plums.
Here the clam deep in the speckled sand.
Are my boots old? Is my coat torn?
Am I no longer young, and still not half-perfect? Let me
keep my mind on what matters,
which is my work,
which is mostly standing still and learning to be
astonished.
The phoebe, the delphinium.
The sheep in the pasture, and the pasture.
Which is mostly rejoicing, since all the ingredients are here,
which is gratitude, to be given a mind and a heart
and these body-clothes,
a mouth with which to give shouts of joy
to the moth and the wren, to the sleepy dug-up clam,
telling them all, over and over, how it is
that we live forever.

—MARY OLIVER[21]

Where "doing" was the headline of past decades, "being" is the larger fuel of life once the years past fifty amass. It doesn't stop

---

21 Mary Oliver. "Messenger," in *Thirst*. (Boston, MA: Beacon Press, 2006).

our activities or contribution: instead it directs and infuses them with joy rather than efforting; trust rather than drive. For many women, this way of seeing/being in one's daily routine has actually become her new statement of purpose.

● *Story* ●

I hadn't planned to interview anyone in their mid-nineties. But then, I didn't expect to meet Allegra Blackwell. Referred by her friend Heather in her eighties, Heather described Allegra as an extraordinary woman with an inimitable smile who would be able to share what's possible up ahead for women. Allegra's picture was included in Heather's email introduction. I noticed her sparkle immediately.

Allegra responded right away to my invitation for an interview. When we connected for the sixty minutes, she generously shared the story of her "most incredible life." A stint in the Navy, then cofounder of a badly needed Head Start program, mother of "two wonderful children," she underwent a life transition when she and her husband moved closer to the mountains. Art, dance, performance, and ceremony overtook previous time spent in early-childhood education. At fifty, she began to travel. Backpacking, climbing, visiting sacred sites, and living with families along the way spoke to Allegra's adventurous nature.

At sixty, she and her husband agreed to divorce, retaining harmony and affection for each other while she traveled and engaged her spiritual development. Allegra came back to the US, bought thirty acres of land at age seventy with friends, and helped build solar-powered houses in which to live.

At eighty-six, Allegra decided to move back to Colorado to be around more people with whom she could connect daily, and where not so much physical labor would be required. Living at a Meditative Retreat Center at the time of our interview, she remained in daily contact with friends, Allegra shared by phone her life lessons and regular practices at ninety-three.

"I want to learn to really love everything and everyone. I know the universe loves me and wants what's best for me. The aging process is so exciting! All my cells are constantly moving—constantly wanting health. Nothing in my body hurts. I have a tremendous amount of energy which comes I think from prana, from within."

Allegra said she doesn't need an alarm clock. Instead, she's "programmed" herself to get up between 5:30 and 7 a.m. every morning—usually at 6 a.m. Upon waking, "I meditate for forty-five minutes with a friend," she said. "Then we do body movements: we move every part of ourselves: hands, ankles, fingers; every part. We face the great rising sun and salute to the four directions, the planets, stars, universe, dimensions; the dimensions of the dimensions. Then we salute our hearts—the most important place. I do Qigong and then go make a meal."

Her other regular practice? "At least once a day—sometimes three or four times—I take naps," she said. "Really important. I lie on the bed with my arms and legs out to make myself more available—like a kid making snow angels. And I go into a different space. I see pictures…sometimes I see words…sometimes it's something I don't know anything about and I really like that. In the evening, I take a walk down the road. Once a week I do meditative spirituality with other women. It helps me grow and know my aversions. It helps me to become. I practice flexing my mind and body."

She became pensive as she concluded, "I am becoming…and I don't know what. But I know we go from one stage to the next, and the whole purpose in life is to unite with ourselves and the Wholeness, the Oneness. We live in order to learn love. And we love so that we can really live.

"We don't need to know anything else."

QUOTES

"It's important to have a private garden in the midst of all the busyness. How to be in alignment with my soul in everything I do—that's what's most important. I'm happier now because it's not about what I'm doing—it's a sustainable feeling of 'It's all here.' Every therapy session I conduct is like an art form; I don't have to plan it all in the way I used to. The preciousness of life and using that in the right way—it's like it's all unfolding."

—ANNIE B., SIXTY-TWO

"Your own joy is the vital sign of your life. You count more than you ever know. You affect more than you'll ever know. You contribute more than you'll ever know. So being who you are well is a good thing to be."

—NORMA J., SIXTY-FIVE

"In many ways I have gone full circle; returning to my childhood when I spent many hours on my own in nature, listening to the trees, the mud, the birds. I've discovered that the hustle and bustle of the world that we think we need in order to be successful is unimportant, really. As the years go on, I'm standing in a way that enables me to embody my 'Self' with humility and understanding. I can tell you that I am finally learning/embodying that 'I am enough just as I am, and I am empowered to do what is mine to do.'"

—FIONA V., SIXTY-THREE

"It's a beautiful journey. Despite the era we are in, future people are going to say we really did make change. Life really is abundant! How blessed we are. In reality, it is all a gift."

—CAROL K., SEVENTY

Antidote To

This Declaration is an antidote to the seductive marketing by our surrounding culture that says satisfaction comes from things that are grand and always outside of ourselves, elusive but for the lucky few. In reality, the exquisite nature of life itself is accessible to all of us on the most ordinary of days.

PRACTICE

To relish something, we need to be ready to notice and have a place to capture what arrives on the soft surface of our hearts.

Find a vase, a bowl, a jar or a wooden box into which you can fit up to fifteen small pieces of paper. In this moment, affirm that there are magically ordinary things that will come into your awareness today. Invite them (right now!) to arrive, and accept that you will see them.

Beginning today, notice at least one "ordinary" thing per day that infuses a moment with sweet awareness. Have a small, neat stack of square-cut papers or post-it notes (in colors perhaps?) ready in an easily accessible area like your kitchen. Know where you can find a pen. The readiness will allow the moment you want to be captured rather than fleeting and forgotten. Right now as I write this, a robin has landed on the pine tree outside my window. She has been motionless for at least two minutes so far, staring squarely into my window, right to where I'm sitting. Now three minutes. Now four...

A robin visited on the backyard pine his morning as I wrote at the dining room table, motionless for a long time, facing me. Felt like a visitation of encouragement! Still here as I write this.

At the end of a two-week period (or one that feels best for your rhythm), reach in and select a few to read and savor. Let them bring into that moment the pleasure of remembering how exquisite life is in all its forms. It's almost like magic, but better.

What will go into your Ordinary Magic jar today?

THINKING FORWARD

WHERE DO WE GO FROM HERE?

This book began with a set of questions—or maybe I should call it a quest. I wanted to explore the groundbreaking ways women fifty to seventy-plus are living a new narrative and breaking through old paradigms. Not only has the big "what now?" question been addressed by 100 women's voices and pioneering steps, but a new blueprint has emerged for me—and I suspect for many other women who can see the exciting shape things are taking right before our eyes. This shape is the reality being lived by millions of women in their fifties, sixties, seventies, and beyond, all around the world. And now, as I close this book, a new question is emerging: "Where do we go from here?"

Of course, looming behind every new question is yet another, especially for interviewers and big-picture people like me. Hence: "And how can we help each other get there?"

As I've pondered these new questions, I've come to believe there are many things we *can* do and *must* do—from everyday conversational shifts we can make to the way media conglomerates portray women and the way we collectively go about voting for our leaders. Some of what we do is so unconscious and deeply embedded that we'll need to exercise new muscles to change it. As we do this, individually and collectively, we will contribute mightily to the new narrative already being written by women over fifty. Our culture is poised for this rewiring.

When I speak of culture, I'd like to frame it as how we behave when people aren't looking. In my organizational development practice when I did corporate culture assessments, I defined culture as "the fly on the wall": Imagine a fly buzzing around our day-to-day world—in this case including work, home, coffee shops, the gym, family gatherings, media, news, social outings, church. What would the fly hear? What might we be saying and doing to *rewrite the narrative* about women who are well over fifty—and putting to rest the worn narrative of yesteryear?

SHIFTING OUR LANGUAGE ABOUT WOMEN OVER FIFTY

Language is one of the things that defines and changes a culture. Acceptable and unacceptable norms are established by it. This includes the ways we speak. What we speak *about*. Who we include as focal points and who we include in the circle of speaking.

Here's what I DON'T want the fly on the wall to overhear when someone is talking with a woman in her fifties, sixties, seventies:

- Are you retired yet?
- When are you planning to retire?
- So what's on your bucket list?
- How are your knees?
- Are you planning any trips in an RV?

- What cruises have you booked?
- Jokes about rocking chairs on front porches.
- Any references to front porches (Read: Sedentary. Aimless. Disengaged from life).
- Assumptions that going to the beach or the golf course is automatically attractive.
- Are you still…*single???* (Asked with trepidation.)
- We can't learn all this new computer stuff! That's for the young people.
- Aging. "Conscious aging," "graceful aging," "healthy aging." (How about "Further Becoming?")
- These golden years aren't so golden.
- We're too old for anyone to listen to us.
- Do you still drive?
- It's really scary out there these days.
- "Seniors" applied to people in their sixties.
- Sixty is the new forty. (No it's not. It's the new sixty.)
- The truth is, life is short.

Here's what I DO want the fly on the wall to overhear when someone is talking to a woman in her fifties, sixties, seventies:

- So, what are you starting up these days?
- I remember that you were thinking about writing a book. How's that going?
- What kind of work are you doing now? Experimenting with anything new?
- What are you doing to stay physically active? I'm looking for new ideas.
- Would you like to have coffee once a month and keep in touch about things that are important in our lives?
- What are you reading that's hopeful and promising about women?

- Have you found a good way to mentor other women? I'm looking for one.
- Since we know women love to have beauty in our lives, what have you found beautiful recently? Is there a way you're creating beauty right now?
- Do you have an Ordinary Magic jar in your kitchen? If not, can I tell you about it?
- Are you expanding your spiritual life in any new ways?
- What's your method of prayer and your way to find hope and inspiration? What practices do you find helpful?
- What are you Done With that I can support you about?
- Do you have any healthy recipes to share? Can I offer you one?
- If you're like lots of women well over fifty you're probably doing something creative in your life, maybe for the first time. Are you painting or singing or learning a musical instrument by any chance?
- Would you be interested in getting a few women together to start a moai?
- What kind of exercise are you doing? I'm looking for new inspiration.
- What's your village/neighborhood like? Have you found a way to create village moments to stay connected to people where you live?
- What are you discovering that's fun these days?
- What have you done for the first time recently?
- What do you find yourself curious about?
- What's your inner voice saying about that? (Related to any issue or dilemma a woman brings up. This is practicing the opposite of giving advice.)

SHIFTING ACTIONS ABOUT WOMEN OVER FIFTY

Of course, changing the culture is not just about the way we speak to—and about—women over fifty. That would put all the burden on us, and we know better than to take that on. Our society also needs to move in the direction of acknowledging and affirming new norms already being seeded by women well over fifty. There are a myriad of ways people and institutions can play a part in reflecting the changing realities and shifting our culture toward the new narrative already arriving. Here are a few ideas:

Here's what I DON'T want the fly on the wall to see related to women in their fifties, sixties, seventies:

- People over fifty depicted on greeting cards as bumbling buffoons.
- Commercials and TV shows associating everyone over sixty with losses: hearing loss, sight loss, memory loss, lost keys. The list goes on and on.
- Community, church, and not-for-profit boards overlooking women in their sixties and seventies for strong roles in leadership.
- Corporate and for-profit boards overlooking women in their sixties and seventies for strong roles in leadership.
- Spoken and unspoken assumptions that women who have stepped out of the workforce don't understand, use, and feel confident with technology.
- Women over sixty shown in mainstream imagery:
  - Sitting in rocking chairs (bored, sedentary)
  - Walking on the beach (no longer useful to or interested in mainstream life)
  - Dancing with their grey-haired spouses in dated living rooms (Yes; a common image. Search free image sites… and shudder.)
  - Hunched over in worry about finances
  - Knitting (need anything be said here?)

- News stories with headlines that depict "the grandmother" who led the protest/ran the marathon/wrote the book/formed a task force. Why are you defining her by her grandchildren? Define her as the powerhouse she is. Use her name. Say what she's doing without reference to her relationships or her age.
- Cashiers, mechanics, plumbers, and service technicians speaking to women over fifty as if they can't understand the homes, cars, and products we've been comparing, purchasing, and maintaining for decades.
- Women over fifty accepting any behavior that feeds the "inevitably invisible" syndrome.
- Employers blind to their formal and informal disclinations to hire persons over fifty for a myriad of unfounded, often unconscious assumptions usually related to energy levels, technological abilities, awareness of current trends, ability to make robust intellectual contributions.
- Travel companies pitching boring packages for women over fifty and sixty that assume no interest in spirited adventure, gritty back-road experiences, high-touch interaction with locals, service, and hardy exercise.
- Images of entrepreneurs on Google coming up 99.9 percent as under forty and male, with nary if ever a woman over fifty-five to be seen (though millions of them are starting new businesses, opening galleries, charting whole new territories as never before).

Here's what I DO want the fly on the wall to see related to women in their fifties, sixties, seventies:

- Media depictions of women over fifty doing the smart, powerful, athletic things they're already doing.
- Women over fifty depicted in movies as intelligent, powerful, socially poised, wise—not centered around seeking a life

partner, navigating failing body parts, or in giddy pursuit of being noticed or wanted romantically by someone.

- Women gathering in moais and acknowledging it's a bit disorienting right now to be at sixty and seventy—not because it's "old" but because we're pioneering something new, and it takes special effort to chart a new course in the absence of firmly established new models.

- All of us generously cheering on any effort another woman makes to be healthy and active.

- All of us applauding any effort another woman makes to do something—anything—for the first time.

- All of us celebrating every public effort other women are making to break the narrative of a downward arc of life. (It doesn't matter if what she does is "successful," it matters that she was willing.)

- Enthusiastically and confidently acknowledging the question "what now?" and respecting people over fifty wanting to reinvent and compose a new segment of life. Bravo the question! From it will come answers.

- All of us reminding our younger sisters that their "be-ing" is as important as their "do-ing"—and not to fall for the patriarchal messaging that suggests we are primarily here to produce, consume, or be party to either.

- Women mentoring other women every chance we get, formally and informally.

- Women experiencing delicious solitude.

- Women finding deep connection with others on a regular basis.

- Women developing a relationship to God and to Self-Witnessing.

- Women recognizing that our sisters of color—Native American, Black, Latina, Asian, and every other category in the minority—have worked exponentially harder to belong and contribute against tremendous odds, and we owe it to ourselves and them to become educated about how true this is. The system is especially dismissive of them and we can help shift the fabric of that reality which currently sub-optimizes everyone.

- Women claiming the best of what "feminine" means as described in this book, without throwing out the best of the masculine. We need both—but we need not tolerate overuse of the masculine. We all should be aiming toward furthering the evolution of goodness, life, truth, and progress.
- Women taking long walks in nature, loving themselves while so doing, and listening for the voice of Spirit speaking to them directly about how needed and important we all are.
- Women being paid equitably with men across the board at all ages.
- A cultural shift politically where women over fifty are overtly sought out—and valued and voted for—because of their maturity and experience.
- Women over fifty leading communities, corporations, and countries.
- Women reading this right now and realizing, no matter what the culture mirrors back, that they are enough just as they are; the Anvil of Their Becoming is valuable beyond measure.

A MEMO TO OUR SURROUNDING CULTURE

To corporate leaders, community boards, politicians, ministers, therapists, senior managers, journalists, funding sources, universities, screenwriters, coaches, policy makers, theatre companies, publishing houses, galleries, and music agencies:

We are here. We are walking forward into a new narrative that we are creating, and we invite you to recognize it as we're architecting it.

We are not waiting to be recognized. Rather, we don't want you to miss out on what's happening right in front of you.

We'd love to have your intelligent partnership as we create a new reality that benefits everyone.

We're inviting. But we're not waiting.

Pay attention.

We are rising.

SUE'S SERVICES

Moai Creation and Support

Coaching

Consulting and Speaking

My Offerings to Women Moving Into Their Further Becoming

Workshops

Further Becoming Workbook

Women's Retreats

Book Group Guide

My Offerings to Women Moving Into Their Further Becoming

Coaching

For guidance, structure, and inspiration to help you create a Pioneer On plan that's unique to you. We'll use the wisdom of the 10 Declarations with an emphasis on doing *and* being.

Workshops

For exploration, discussion, and application of the 10 Declarations to your life in a circle of like-minded women. Face-to-face and online available.

Women's Retreats

If you want the full package! Deep-dive visioning into the next phase of your life using Scenario Possibilities™; R&R in a stunning setting to feed your soul; experienced facilitation and a circle of like-minded women who will become your tribe for one year of continued connection.

Book Group Guide

For rich discussion and application of the 10 Declarations with your circle of women readers.

Further Becoming Workbook

A self-paced workbook offering reflection and practice exercises to support your Further Becoming journey in the privacy of your own process.

Consulting and Speaking

For groups and organizations poised to support women to live fully into this time of life, uplifting and enlivening keynotes and consultation.

Moai Creation and Support

Every woman deserves to belong to a moai! Support for launching and providing your own facilitation of a moai with other women to add deeper relating and connecting into your life.

ACKNOWLEDGMENTS

I'm grateful to feel this grateful. It means I've had the gift of many people entering my life, touching and changing me in the most unexpected ways at times, and supporting my Further Becoming.

First, I want to thank the 100 women I interviewed who so generously shared the stories of their lives. Every one of their voices is included in this book, either quoted or through the spirit of what she shared. Each time I finished a phone interview, I felt expanded with hope, awe, humble appreciation, and enlarged energy. With these women and others like them who are influencing the trajectory of our world, there is hope for our continued evolution toward what is good and life-giving for all. Their resilience and wisdom have touched me more deeply than I can say and literally changed my life. I'm thrilled to pass along their inspiration for other women to hear.

I also want to thank my coaching clients, past and present, whose lives I'm deeply privileged to witness and support as they further compose their life journeys.

As I reflect on my life-changing teachers and mentors, the lines blur in all the ways they have supported me. My spiritual growth has always been of primary importance, so I owe endless gratitude to RRM. Other practitioners have also catalayzed defining break-throughs in my view of reality. My heart holds abiding gratitude to JE, TF, CV, ED, and NG. Some names are meant to remain private, but you know who you are!

I'm immensely grateful to the primary professional teacher of my career, Fred Kofman. His work in conscious business defined twenty-five years of my consulting and coaching practice. Shell Oil company was the vehicle through which I had the opportunity to train with Fred. Via Cindy Miller's transformational leadership, I was also delivered opportunities to be trained by Peter Senge, Rick Ross, Margaret Wheatley, Otto Scharmer, and Dawna Markova. Their work informs mine to this day. Later, Cindy Wigglesworth's groundbreaking work on spiritual intelligence, Terri O'Fallon's work on human development, and Jeff Salzman's unparalleled application of integral theory have fueled my growth and practice.

I could not have continued this book project without the support, love, cheering, and savvy insights from my loved moai sisters Sandra Zimmer and Mary Beth McEuen. They along with Kathie Magness and Peter Haskell in the past, have taught me the power of sisterhoods from which I was able to write a related chapter. I was also supported and cheered on by the wisdom, brilliant insights, and caring of my colleague and friend Barbara Alexander, along with Beth Macy and Susan Furness who joined an advisory group for this book early on. Kirsten Wilson, beloved young Batia, Fiona Henderson, my cousins Sue Koch and Joan Fischer, Sweet Birch lifelong friends Karole and Jean, and my tribe of dear friends all leaned in with interest and support in ways I deeply appreciate. I'm also grateful for Betsy's years of tender sisterhood in my life, and for Maggie's present ones.

There are no words to express my respect and endless appreciation for the partnership I experienced working with my editor, Gail Hudson. Her skilled review of this book along the way, her savvy precision for knowing where things needed expansion or excision, her wisdom as a deeply grounded woman who "got" this book and its message, provided me with exactly the expertise and support I needed. Without her, this book would not be what it is.

I'm grateful to Nikki Van De Car who helped me chisel the initial Declarations, for the background support of Alexandra Oliver and Stacie Velehradsky, and for Kelly Notaras's book *The Book You Were Born to Write* which provided practical and oh-so-helpful tips on birthing one's book as a new author. Trina Brunk's intuitive artistry brought early depictions of the Ten Declarations to life in a way that I could see and engage. And Ginger Kern and Jordan Martindell assisted me with their uncanny organizational skills which helped me stay sane as I tracked permissions and interview details.

My beloved dad Frederick Brightman cannot go without mention. A huge example of what a meaningful life looks like, he modeled how to continue contributing to the world and what daily personal and spiritual growth looks like. He is with me every day through the values that guide me. My brother Fred is also a shining model of what it looks like to "throw off the old" and continue becoming through scholarly pursuits, unfailing commitment to spiritual priorities, and discipline.

I'm grateful for my mother pioneering our family's introduction and study of a theology that was new to us and redefined how we understand the universe, including all mankind.

And last but not least, my life was forever changed when my

children Lilly and Sam entered it. I cannot put into words how they have shaped every day of my life with greater truth, artistry, goodness, and love.

Looking ahead, I appreciate every reader who will take pieces of the 100 women's inspiring voices and continue her own Further Becoming—a blessing to herself and the world.

QUOTED WORKS

"Messenger" from the volume *Thirst* by Mary Oliver, published by Beacon Press, Boston. Copyright © 2004 by Mary Oliver, used herewith by permission of the Charlotte Sheedy Literary Agency, Inc.

"A Valley Like This" from *Even in Quiet Places* by William Stafford. Copyright © 1996 by The Estate of William Stafford. Reprinted with the permission of The Permissions Company, LLC on behalf of Confluence Press, confluencepress.com.

Long Life: Essays and Other Writings by Mary Oliver, copyright © 2004. Quoted excerpt reprinted by permission of Da Capo Press, an imprint of Hachette Book Group, Inc.

"Ah, Not To Be Cut Off" from *Selected Poetry of Rainer Maria Rilke*, translation copyright © 1995 by Stephen Mitchell; edited and translated by Stephen Mitchell. Used by permission of Random House, an imprint and division of Penguin Random House LLC. All rights reserved.

ABOUT THE AUTHOR

SUE BRIGHTMAN is the founder and president of Women on the Journey of Their Lives, LLC, an enterprise dedicated to supporting women over fifty through coaching, purpose retreats, and inspirational advocacy through teaching, speaking, and writing. In 2015, Sue began researching the newly emerging state of Adulthood II by conducting 100 interviews with women in their fifties, sixties, and seventies. Inspired by the exciting new tracks women at this stage are laying down for generations to come, she wrote this book to offer new models to women everywhere. A Conscious Business trainer and coach for twenty-five years prior, Sue has provided consulting and leadership development to some of the world's largest organizations through Brightman Glover International, a company she founded in 2000. She is a certified spiritual intelligence coach through Deep Change, Inc.; a volunteer interfaith chaplain for community criminal justice and mental health institutions; and now combines her business expertise, spiritual practice, and women-specific research into her work with individuals and groups.